# SPARKS FROM LIFE'S FLINT

## Meditations for the Future Soul, Today

by

Todd Green

*Sparks from Life's Flint: Meditations for the Future Soul, Today* is a publication of GreenLight Productions, 1352 Judy Street, Minden, NV 89423, 1-888-568-1282. Website: www.toddgreen.com; E-mail: trg@toddgreen.com

Cover Illustration: Agni Yoga by Nicholas Roerich (1874 – 1947) Use by kind permission from Nicholas Roerich Museum, New York, NY, Website: www.roerich.org

Cover Design by Alyssa Angelis

ISBN: 0-9777854-0-8

Printed in the United States of America
First printing 2006

**Dedicated to the Memory of
John and Florence Green
and Joey**

Religions are many and different from one another, but only in form. Water is one and the same element, and formless, only it takes the shape of the channel which holds it and which it uses for its accommodation; and so the name water is changed to river, lake, sea, stream, pond, etc. So it is with religion; the essential truth is one, but the aspects are different.

*Hazrat Inayat Khan*


I go into the Muslim mosque and the Jewish synagogue and the Christian church and I see one altar.

*Rumi*

# TABLE OF CONTENTS

## SPIRITUAL AWAKENING

## HEALTH & WHOLENESS

# TRUTH & FREEDOM

# CREATIVITY

# LOVE & RELATIONSHIPS

## NATURE

# PREFACE

You hold in your hands a creation begun most unexpectedly in the summer of 2003. I attempted to write a little ditty for a sweet neighbor (an amateur poet himself) to iron out a misunderstanding we were having. That one short poem opened up a floodgate of inspiration, leading to the writing of more than a thousand poems over the course of a year and a half.

Through experimenting with lots of standard formats, I found the sonnet to be the one that I particularly enjoyed. (Most of the poems in this edition are in that format.) Sonnets are traditionally fourteen lines in what is called iambic pentameter with a variety of rhyming patterns like ABAB, CDCD, EFEF, GG or ABBA, CDDC, EFEFEF or ABBA, ACCA, DEDE, FF, etc.

As an aid to those of you who have not read a lot of poetry, it is important to get a sense of the rhythm of each poem. Once you tap into that and maintain it throughout, its message will find a deeper place to germinate within your heart. Other aids are enunciating the words very clearly in your mind or, even better, saying them out loud. Good rhythm and clear diction will bring into focus more intently the meaning of the words and phrases.

This set of poems has been roughly divided into the chosen subject areas, but there is also a lot of crossover where a specific poem could have easily been in a different chapter. Some of the placements may seem arbitrary, which they probably are. The poems are placed alphabetically within the chapters in order to facilitate finding favorite ones. I have taken it upon myself to place a few definitions in a glossary, where I felt they may be needed. Any word with an asterisk is defined. As you become more familiar with the subjects of the poems, you will notice similar topics advanced. Important points, submitted different ways, are intended to help you the reader gain a better understanding.

Concerning the term Christ as it is used in some of these poems: Try not to get hung up on whether it refers to the personage of Jesus or a Universal Ideal that we all aspire to. Read it in the context that you feel most comfortable with. Some poems you may agree with, some you may not, and some may seem to make no sense. Run with the ones that resonate within you and "place on the shelf", for the time being, those others. Use the ones you enjoy as a foundation and remember: Little keys unlock the biggest doors.

Though the discipline of poetry is relatively new for me, the concepts expounded upon in these poems are not. I have had a lifelong interest in comparative religion and metaphysics, the 'whys' of life. This project turned into a wonderful way to share these discoveries with others. I hope you enjoy these as much as I enjoyed writing them, for what is life but a voyage of discovery?

Finally, I would like to acknowledge the support, both inner and outer, for this work. Mark L. Prophet (1919 – 1973), a Western mystic and visionary author and lecturer, who founded the Summit Lighthouse; Hazrat Inayat Khan (1882 – 1927), a master Indian musician and pioneer in the communication of the Sufi philosophy to the West; George Oshawa (1893 – 1966), writer and the founder of Macrobiotic principles and lifestyle practices. I have only 'met' these great men through their printed and recorded words, but the beauty of their souls lives on. And last, but definitely not least, is my beloved wife, Sarolta, whose love, support, tireless work at the computer and thoughtful suggestions helped immeasurably to bring this book to fruition. Enjoy!

# I
# Spiritual Awakening

## A Love Supreme

O living flame of sacred love so pure
Cast upon a mortal frame of light
Wisdom balanced with power and love's the cure
A pillar of truth raised up in sacred rite
Clear, whole, pure, radiant love
Spins the wheels to raise the soul beyond
Beyond this mortal veil to God above
With calls afire, His blessed hosts respond
A peace within begets goodwill towards man
Sacrifice and honor make one whole
The sacred part of the puzzle to charge His plan
A tireless joy that clarifies the goal
We're each a vital point of a love supreme
Making tangible and whole His blessed dream

## A Peaceful Heart

Joy exudes from a peaceful heart
Silent and commanding
From life's daily fray, it stands apart
Benignly thus demanding

Within the heaven of heavens it does shine
Its sheltering arms held wide
The measure of how our wholeness is defined
With harmony fore'er allied

The soul does call it king with purity's grace
Serene contemplation
Silence within the aura's hallowed space
Strife's demarcation

Soundness in the body, heart and mind
Complete integration
Perfect flow, all's sacredly entwined
The heart of purification

## A Sense of Wholeness

To sense the unfolding 'round duration's bend
Gives all things a blessed, radiant glow
A sense of grace and peace can now descend
God-perfection's touching here below
Blissful is the sensing of His presence
Symmetry is the passkey to His land
Wholeness is to ever touch His essence
Weaving our ascension garment, strand by strand
Circumstance in truth, plays no part
Expansion occurs beyond all space and time
An awareness of 'here' and 'there' becomes the start
The unfolding of mastery's order, so sublime
Carry a sense of wholeness where'er you go
Radiating sacred light from head to toe

## A Variable State of Blind

Whichever direction you turn, you see the vision
The vision of the One, manifest
All variables are found in our decision
These decisions made become life's ultimate test
For all blooms from a single cosmic stem
Healing of all conflict's in our merging
As all are found as "I", not as "them"
God restores completeness through His purging
Unity's found when life's lived true and real
Nothing's known beyond His presence whole
It's through the breaking of His covenant seal
That the mind's illusions cloud our goal
Let vision pure become our state of mind
All else becomes a variable state of blind

## All We Are

For all the holiness we have thus acquired
Counts for nothing in the scheme of things
The most important element that's required
Is the sharing of the purity that it brings
Being self-absorbed will lead to nowhere
Our spirit stagnates when there is no flow
Our good that's stored in heaven's nearly bare
How much we give to life is how we grow
But gains will only come when keeping silent
Silent as the world before each dawn
The more we grow the less we will resent
For what we give away's not really gone
Take all we are and give it to the Lord
Life returns with interest what's outpoured


## Arise!

Arise each soul on wings
Enraptured, now ascend
Praise to our good Lord
As every heart does mend

All good and all beneficence
With glory does appear
When we seek His center
And to His will adhere

All life's antecedent*
Is our God unseen
Creation sun ablaze
Yet blessed and serene

By silence and through void
All that is appears
Cycles within cycles
Spheres within spheres

Power and holy wisdom
Love's natal source
Guiding each pliant soul
On salvation's course

Raised up by His grace
To perfection's height
His glorious radiance dazzles
Our humble mortal sight

Almighty God within
All wond'rous works are Thine
Imbued with holy wisdom
His love does purely shine

Though these glorious wonders
Are so scant explored
The portion we've been blessed with
Each heart has so adored

Infinite love so prescient
Does quicken humble eyes
All the soul does need
His glorious path provides

Throughout His blest creation
Be still and hear His voice
It tingles and exhilarates
Our soul does so rejoice

Call forth His mighty hosts
That they may descend
A healing and a comfort
Their presence does transcend

Glory filled with gratitude
As each does bow in praise
His constant love transforms
The heart to thus upraise

## The Art of Prayer

Praying without ceasing
Conundrum of the ages
God's law of increasing
Pursued by saints and sages

For life's a living prayer
Depends on how you address it
It starts with are you aware
Each moment, thus possess it

All prayers are made of words
But words are symbols for
Qualities to rouse or gird
To heal, judge or adore

By the mastering of prayer's art
Those qualities you become
When praying's heart to Heart
You become their sum

## Beautiful View

Peace be still, to know the Lord our God
His splendiferous blessings are bestowed
O lesser one upon this mortal sod
Turn the dial, tune in the heavenly mode
The tingling of a blessed peace within
Realigns, our mortal vision, clear
Never again to be what we have been
His blessings so magnificent and dear
Each moment now so rife with perfect joy
The perfection of a pure transfusing hue
These words aren't meant to seem just plain or coy
But an explication of a beautiful view
The bumps of life are smoothed by perfect love
Perfect love, come down from God above

### Become Absorbed

So oft in lonely towns and mid the din
In times of weariness with sensations spent
God's shores of silence beckon to each one
Come within and start your soul's ascent
Supernal silence, the comfort of the soul
Unfathomed peace, the place of great delight
The vital speaking presence of His spirit
The soul is in its perfect place aright
Sweet love, is the magic of beyond
With stillness, perfect joy and perfect peace
Beyond mere words, sensations of eterne
The only prayer is, "God, may You increase"
Become absorbed, with senses left behind
Limitless are the blessings that you'll find

### Become the Word

It's the power and fire behind the voice
That quivers the ethers allowing one to hear
Purifying the soul to affect its choice
Expanding love to cast out doubt and fear
Reciting rote can't ever know the depth
Of the soul's petition to God's heart
But is the vigilance that that one has kept
Infused with Holy Spirit from the start?
What we create anew, each petition
No vacant, bland recital of the word
Alert and present is the pre-position
Essential tools thus needed to be heard
Add joy, to this wisdom of the age
To become the Word, we must engage

# Been There, Done That

Those, since the ancient ages came
Up to the present in these latter days
We all depart in our special ways
But in a sense, our journeys are the same

This our home of earth, sea and sky
Is not eternally here for anyone
We all depart in truth as we have come
As generations follow, by and by

We each make our entrance, many a time
Equal exits as the curtain drops
What is real we take, not earthly props
The soul upon life's spiraling steps does climb

For most, life is cloaked in outer mystery
Toiling in this crucible of life
Impiety reigns in these halls of strife
To these the afterlife's a wait-and-see

The coarsened must have life then tutor them
No learning or maturing as a soul
Though growth, in truth, should be their only goal
There's no nimbus*, just a thorny diadem*

We each and all have had so many mothers
Sisters, brothers and many fathers too
Souls worldwide still hold this point of view
Though life will always let you have your druthers*

Lessons learned, momentums gained, accrue
But many, though, will never really get it
The blind leading the blind becomes the culprit
For ages, all their fallacies they bestrew

The Christian faith at one time did accept
Reincarnation, a part of holy writ
But early on, church fathers did omit
This ancient tenet and profound concept

One blind, one whole, one lame, right from birth
There's no justice anyone can see
Brought upon each soul by God-decree
Past rights and wrongs, carried down to earth

As one excels in this and one in that
Each got started well before they came
Our strengths and faults will never be the same
Our good and bad repaid, tit for tat

The tenet of every faith: "Do unto others
As you would have them do, unto you"
The greatest truth if all would follow through
See all upon life's path as holy brothers

We're one, created from a common source
Distinctive drops drawn from a mighty sea
Our full potential's loving pedigree
We play our part in life, God's tour-de-force

### Blessed Silence

Blessed silence so pure, sing to me
Beat upon my whorled and weary ears
Transform me to thy realms that I may be
Filled with 'music' that my soul may hear
Lips be still, be thee calm and mum
Stable, fixed as heaven's curfew sent
It's from this source that all surrenders come
And how the soul's made sweet and eloquent
God speaks through this silence cast within
Echoes through the quietude and peace
But mindless chatter has the hue of din
Clamoring on, His voice then fades to cease
Be vigilant with the words that you would say
They'll be the cross you'll have to bear someday

### The Bud and the Bulb

Why would we, Spirit's grand creation
Be hallowed any less than bud and bulb
These perennial displays show us resurrection
Just as all the mystics have foretold

Starting in the spring of our lifeline
Followed by the summer of life's abundance
Reaping autumn's fruit as energies decline
Towards winter's ending of this cosmic dance

If the life-force of the bloom and leaf
Returns to God's good Terra once again
Would you deny the soul through wrong belief
A reappearance to earn her* diadem?


### By Your Grace

I surrender, and accept Your sacred trust
For trusting is the light that never fails
Melt with love this hardened human crust
That I may serve to balance this life's scales
Who am I without Your noble love?
A meager mortal shell of skin and bone
The breath of life infuses from above
As grievances I faithfully atone
I surrender, raise me from this space
This mortal clay of density and pain
With crystallized radiance, now replace
All that's been the not-self's* ball and chain
I'll now abide in a life that's real and true
For by Your grace I've finally got a clue

## Childlike Equals Christlike

Most, never leave the childish state
Though living to a ripened senior age
A revolving door instead of heaven's gate
Till soul maturity there's still another page
But don't confuse childish with childlike
With simplicity, it's the way of God
How to garner the innocence of a tyke?
The path to wisdom every soul must trod
Sincere words and actions are never lost
Truthfulness, more prized than any knowledge
An intuition one simply can't exhaust
Accreditation not found at any college
The childlike mind is how to enter in
To the Christic mind, it's most akin


## Christic Key to Life

Through many centuries of wearing imperfection
Mingled with relative states of perfected good
Our burdens and problems need introspection
All reality's contained in our selfhood
The errors man has committed are often considered
A viciousness having its origin outside himself
In time it makes them hostile or embittered
The links 'tween sowing and reaping remain stealth
There are no maladies anywhere God's created
It's energy man's negated in various forms
When this is understood, strife is abated
For resistance drives the winds of emotional storms
If initiations in life are clearly assessed
Then the Christic key to life's possessed

## The Cosmic Ratio

Man in reality's a manifest being of light
But his innate assets are untapped
Trapped between the earthly and divine
He needs his God-potential now unstrapped

Content to stand in vain anticipation
It seems so hard abiding in this search
Again to settle toward capitulation
With its lies all purity it does besmirch

The plains of Sodom then don't look so bad
As compared to this arduous path of escape
In fact, the heights of truth are easier to scale
Than the slippery slope of a base landscape

By inner determination we clear a path
Shutting out the clamor of human propensity
A faith in the all-enduring truth sustains
Till the soul's raised up from all its density

A vow thus taken to turn toward heaven's way
To walk with God, seeing all potential
It's not a given, for God requires proof
Through life's trials, fathom what's essential

The tests we face are for the mastery of self
A reaping of the harvest that we've sown
When debts are paid and consciousness is pure
God's door is opened, showing we have grown

Wither can we go without His presence?
There's no time or place He is not so
For wherever love and truth are, there God is
Bestowing full potential to then grow

There's no evil in the mind of God
But light's defined through every human monad*
This power enables man, through his free will
To create the veil in which he now is clad

13

For God provided awareness with identity
But knowledge of good and evil, He forbade
Deemed moot, to the evolving of His reality
And for our walk in paradise, a fair trade

Man through free will, tasted of this knowledge
Which caused a mighty schism from within
His human pride became his faulty lighthouse
Lighting a pathway to his final ruin

Whatever man conceives, he can create
Good or evil borne upon his soul
All that he creates is of God's energy
The secret's in discovering life's true goal

By every wrong decision, we have densified
Moved away then from our source of light
By perverting our free will, ill abounds
Brooking evil's lies, we've lost our birthright

Till once again, when each of us does show
A willingness and humility to choose right
We'll flounder about then in life's astral* sea
Till God alone is held within our sight

This place most high, this paradise of old
A place we earn the right to walk anew
We're each a drop come forth then from His ocean
Though "Ye are gods"* is modern faith's taboo

In reality, it's the key from which life's built
We 'ocean drops', co-create with light
This truth's beheld just 'yond our sin and guilt
Till we're shown approved then in His sight

We're inheritors of His realm of love
Our home before this trek in earthly woe
It's life's true goal, most worthy then for all
As we balance our cosmic ratio

## Divine Direction

The paucity of a language thus portrays
The outer surface of supernal truth
Its beauty is demeaned by trite clichés
An innocence not cognized since our youth
The surety of a faith endowed with grace
Sanctified vision with the inner eye
The blending of one's inner and outer space
The flow of reality will never mystify
Becoming one with God does raise the soul
To infinite realms of truth and inner peace
Realigning to a permanent goal
As confusion and anxiety wane and cease
Wholeness is the sign of Christ-perfection
Open the heart to sense divine direction


## Divine Initiation

Be constant and tenacious for the Lord
With love, they're the nature of His way
Free from pride, they sound a perfect chord
They're the keynote of the Christ to now portray
Moving at a self-determined pace
Initiation's the governor of our speed
But Christic imitation helps erase
The self-imposed restrictions that impede
By daily application to our attainment
We open transcendent doors till now unseen
The clarity gleaned, from this pure ordainment
Purifies till now what's been unclean
Life's events aren't held in isolation
All's a part of divine initiation

## Don the Royal Robes

Energy's misspent on our passing fashions
Instead, consider God's eternal raiment
Garments of brilliance tailored by heaven's angels
Serving life becomes the binding payment
Cosmic vestments bound for eternal glory
Habiliments* garnered with seven* sacred jewels
Rays of perfection cast a radiant glow
Bands of light reveal our sacred accrual
Too many take their pleasure in tattered garb
A varied wardrobe of confusion, mist and haze
Paltry attire quite similar to many others
Its material poorly made by human malaise
Why wear the rags of astral* discontent?
Don the royal robes of Christ's ascent

## The Dweller's Claw

We've all got a dweller* or not-self
Filled with cunning and guile
Not a heavenly aspect
But a part that's baleful and vile

As we each day pray or decree
Cleaned of our burdens and woe
By re-immersing in the world
We employ what God's made so

But notice that voice within
Giving its OK to dabble
Dragging His light through the mud
Through squalor and all of its scrabble

By giving God just a moment
An occasional time and place
There's a balance we while away
His blessings we thus debase

We say, what's a little indulgence?
A little bit here and there
I can stop any time
I'll never get trapped or ensnared

This voice of human compromise
Of carnal lies and deceit
Gets the soul to take wrong turns
Preying on mortal conceit

We're so easily led astray
With no discernment of the soul
Subtly twisting the mind
And spiritually taking its toll

Then, before we know it
We're back where we began
This indulging left unchecked
Separates us from God's plan

Thinking this way is right
Will in the end lead to death
Not some religious hyperbole
But truth, its sum and breadth

Living with holiness and sanctity
The burden that is light
Within His flame of glory
Our not-self's now in flight

Let conscience be the guidepost
"Do unto others" become our law
Live simply and live humbly
To stay out of the dweller's claw

## Eternal Models

Our earth's played host to many hearts of love
Who dedicated their all to serve the light
They tied their souls below to God above
Through His truth they tried to set things right
These efforts were the basis of their call
Done with abundant love and pure audacity
Their goal to restore what was before the fall
Standing for truth, in this age of mendacity*
These blessed souls were not all of renown
Though nothing could obscure their beck and call
No matter what, they would receive their crown
Overcoming every hurdle and pit fall
Study the experiences of these blessed ones
Eternal models of God's blessed Son

## The Eternal Paradigm

This womb of sound
So real and profound
Is the source of all that we know
All comes from it
This cosmic summit
As our light bodies expand and grow

Now is forever
Forever is now
All that is, has always been
Divinity's reign
The dweller's* bane
Perfect, or we try it again

Heaven's perfection
No human detection
Only found by the pure of heart
No doubt and fear
Will ever appear
If from God we never depart

When rites and rituals
Descend to habitual
Done to the soul's dismay
Alert and awake
All vanity forsake
Truth is what we portray

There's a time and a pace
A realm and a space
Where the soul is fulfilled and sublime
But that time has no pace
That realm has no space
For now is the eternal paradigm

## Expect the Best

If we're immersed in negative thought and word
That's what we out-picture
As part of the human herd
The result is we expect the worst
Counterfeit coin found in our purse
God's flow of good is stopped by human stricture

Whatever color we then paint life, it's that
Within becomes without
It's just what we begat
Co-creators with God are we
The law of life by God-decree
Let our life be blessed, pure and devout

If we're immersed in positive thought and word
That's what then outplays
The spirit does engird*
The result is we expect the best
Wholly free, not like the rest
We're now attuned with heaven's blest arrays

## Feeling Mighty Blessed

Nothing in life's more challenging or more fruitful
Than the path of initiation we're placed upon
Thread by thread, only we can create
The coat of many colors we will don
Each soul, in truth, is where it needs to be
Where we are is the fruit of many lives
Less rebellion will help us better see
Inner growth does come to those who strive
Life's initiations are how we move
Up or down the ladder moves our soul
Banging off life's walls or in the groove
Being broken or growing much more whole
The choice is ours to pass or fail our tests
Bowed by life or feeling mighty blessed

## Find Your Passion

Be trusting of the graces of our Lord
Let the fire within be the exemplar
Our calling's what will lead us ever onward
Divine love's the essence of His nectar
But prayers of dry intent bear no response
God sees to our heart-flame's very core
Want of constancy finds one in defiance
His sacred voice says, "Whom do you adore?"
Be made a vessel yielding of the Lord
A beautiful life's of little things done well
When we find our passion we're not bored
As doubt and human questioning are expelled
Our life is all a blessing from on high
Through good works, that blessing multiplies

## Fruits of Faith

Hear, O souls of tepid faith, stand tall!
By our lack of faith we slight the Lord
Our simple act of trust will sure forestall
The onset and the growth of all discord
Experience reflects what's found inside our selves
All's within the circle of our being
Clues come forth when into life one delves
Then God illumines by an inner seeing
One may be engulfed by myriad events
Set to test the mettle of our soul
Not holding the immaculate concept's what foments
Our mishaps place us deeper in the hole
When events in life seem dour, cold and bleak
That's when the fruits of faith must surely speak

## Giving God the Glory

Regard all service and sacrifice that's made
Not as a means of success or recognition
But as a sacred shovel and sacred spade
Tilling the ground of truth, life's pure ambition
No amount of worldly wealth or fame
Will cleanse a stain that's cast upon the soul
Heavenly wealth and glory's not the same
A different set of rules and final goal
The joy of inner peace will take its time
Realigning energies gone askew
But ceding it for outer gain's a crime
Heaven's gold for tainted revenue
When service becomes a virtue in our eyes
Giving God the glory's how it complies

## God of Love

When weighing what motivates us to move
Exactly what's the rudder that helps us steer
By taking notice it will surely prove
Whether that factor's based in love or fear
Too many today who profess the common faith
Use angst as a motivating force
While awaiting the coming Christic wraith
From love's reality they are now divorced
But fear in any matrix is a poison
Contaminating all found pure and whole
Stunting all the potential of God's foison*
And for the aspirant a debilitating toll
Fear of God's the living of a lie
A God of love, all life does dignify


## God Will Determine

How much we presuppose now through our pride
Our efforts seen as noble and so grand
The carnal mind is taking us for a ride
As our ego answers its command
Thinking our good effort's worth a prize
One much bigger than we've thus far earned
This narrow thought begets a sad surprise
The weight we feel, shows we haven't learned
From where we are we cannot make the call
Of where we're standing in the eyes of God
Our presumption's now our life's pitfall
His reality's not this vain façade
With diligent faith keep on to work and pray
God will determine our reparation day

## God, The One

All God's spangled host
Touch the soul inmost
Touch this secret place with hallowed fire
Such a perpetual peace
Sanctified release
To higher vistas may the soul aspire
Wholeness of a unity trine
A Christic heart, the sacred shrine

But out-picturing ingratitude
And adding an aloof attitude
Surely takes one's spirit off life's course
For egocentric bane
Causes spiritual pain
In truth, there's no acknowledgement of the source
God, the one, the celestial sun
The wellspring of our victories won

## God's Perfection Manifest

Throughout creation, both great and small
We see perfection, our God in all
In miracles He brings forth each spring
It's everywhere and everything

His perfect work is all around
Sense its beauteous sights and sound
I AM* proclaims in earth and sky
And in our origin, perfection's die*

God has sent His radiant Son
That our ascension could be won
Each day, gives a chance for man
To pass life's tests, fulfill God's plan

Though we may suffer, still try and try
Through our victory, life sanctify
That God may grant each in His time
An eternal life found most sublime

## God's Sacred Way

We're like a farmer with his bounteous field
Rows to hoe before we sow our seed
We trust in God, for the future yield
It's in His hands, we each then must concede
For we, like the farmer, cannot say
We'll decide just when our field bears fruit
When seedlings will flourish on which day
As every other desire follows suit
Know all we do is faithfully sow the seed
Then trust in God that it will germinate
It's the laws of life, God's holy creed
These cosmic laws, He'll not abrogate*
Let all we do be done God's sacred way
Where're we turn, this truth is on display

## Good Works

Does not our soul possess the sacred flame?
Which all upon our verdant home hold true
Arise, let all become what is the same
Pure passion as each heart receives its due
Celestial angels in mortal forms appear
Their cosmic beauty comes from higher realms
Serving man through service so sincere
Victory as His flame does overwhelm
They draw in all the bright, immortal fire
Holding true to visions held within
Each moment seems to take them ever higher
That we in time may see our home again
Boundless as all sing, His love made whole
Good works accrued upon the karmic* scroll

## Hear the Inner Voice

Prompts are what life gives to guide our way
But we won't e're be driven against our will
For subtle is God's style on every ray*
Inner attunement is what He would instill
But toil is the bent of humankind
So many seem oblivious to cosmic laws
Bouncing off the walls of life purblind
With nary an understanding of the cause
Sleepwalking as we seek a compromise
Devising all our petty human schemes
What next will the carnal mind devise?
Better to seek the path that so redeems
Rediscover life's original sacred oath
Hear the inner voice of divinity's growth


## Heavenly Skies

Hear the joyous sound of love
Budding as your heart's desire
It's God's glorious sound attire
The soul's awakened as a dove

Where valor kindles, virtue lies
Naught to else but God hath faith
Our soul, once one, does now retrace
A path that leads to heavenly skies

## Heaven's Blueprint

Start to develop such a heart of love
And give that love to all who count on you
Let it spread to all, here and above
There's no part of life we then eschew
For God may sound us out at any time
What in life prevents our jumping in?
Will He find us balanced, whole and prime?
Or under a sea of woe as life's has-been
Such love shouldn't count on anyone
To reciprocate that love in any way
Its source is an eternal dawning sun
Giving to all of life's that soul's forte
The love of God enables all to grow
Serving is heaven's blueprint here below


## Heaven's Charm

The touch of heaven's charm
A blessing and a gift
Its clarity and its wholeness
Gives the soul a lift

Such a purity of purpose
Raises life within
We're as living flames
To sacred love akin

The thralldom of the senses
In no way can compare
When we so attune
To this heavenly prayer

## His Cosmic Sign

The beauty of a heart that's filled with love
Exudes a grace that's mystically divine
As His presence radiates from above
Life takes on a multi-dimensional shine
Truth's endowed with a cosmic flame
A flame aglow found in a humble heart
Truth and love are intrinsically the same
From this unity never should one part
To expand and create, transforming who we are
A child of God ennobled by His peace
Becoming one, with our inner star
It's how divinity takes on a true increase
The sooner we discover we're divine
The sooner God unveils His cosmic sign

## His Glory Manifest

There's naught a day in life that we don't breathe
Excepting but the day that is our last
Being is what breath does then bequeath
A strictured life or one that's infinitely vast

There's naught a day in life that we don't see
Excepting those whose eyes are stricken blind
But using inner sight will help us Be
To seize the promise of the cosmic mind

There's naught a day in life that we don't hear
Excepting those who detect no outer sounds
But all have a gift to use their inner ear
Hearing the voice of God that so abounds

There's naught a day in life that we can't love
Excepting those who consciously shut the fount
This infinite fount's our wellspring from above
But we affect its quality and amount

So whether we like it or not, we're all here
Here each day to witness or debase
We summon the type of day that will appear
Our will determines the qualities we embrace

Don't let another moment e'er be wasted
Through petty worry or simple human doubt
Never another moment we've not tasted
The sweetness of God's nectar all about

There's naught another day that we'll not breathe
See, hear and sense His glorious way
Then all reality He will so enwreathe
With the perfection of His full bouquet

We've then become our God, who's within
The fullness of His glory manifest
No more the sleeping soul that we have been
For God has now endowed us, whole and blessed


**His Heavenly Reward**

The story of our God, is our story
A tale of the soul attaining light
The glory of our God, is our glory
The fulfillment of the law, our sacred right
For Deity is a presence, wholly pure
Who endows all with His sacred flame
As the soul gets stronger and mature
The mantle of His presence, it will claim
For God, by His grace, helps one endure
Clears our vision to better see our way
For all that ails in life He is the cure
His will, by true humility, we do obey
Glory in the blessings of the Lord
A peace within, His heavenly reward

## His Mighty Way

Let freedom's aspirant admit to his potential
Shattering the old matrix
Esteeming what's essential
A true respect for His guidelines
Upon this path that life assigns
Rejecting all our dweller's* guile and tricks

The hurling of anathema* by mankind
Seems today a part
Of the worldly mind
The practices of the saints and sages
Called weird or senseless through the ages
There's no sense of the truth He does impart

But worldly fashions today are far more foolish
Than seeking His good grace
Their vanity makes them mulish
Wear well the garb of piety
Based in practicality
The Christic path that all may then retrace

For God's qualities are adornments 'yond compare
A multitude of gifts
Accessed through sincere prayer
Wisdom, love, devotion, fervor
Sweetness, strength, an aspiring server
With a constant faith in God that ever lifts

Express the faith and order all may wear
No hint of human snobbery
A sordid, vain affair
Pursue the wisdom of God's plan
Seek no glory from mortal man
This path is not the way of cosmic jobbery*

Esteem God's will and not the views of men
They're the same old story
Retold and told again
But the power of His mighty way
No human views can rock or sway
We're molded in His radiant love and glory

## Impassioned Communion

Our Lord abides so deep within the heart
Superficial calls won't get one there
If you're wondering why you seem apart
Maybe there's no passion in your prayer
Memorized recitation's just skin deep
The listening angels will hardly give a notice
Inflamed with the Holy Spirit will help you reap
As a Buddha on a thousand-petaled lotus
The more impassioned are our heartfelt prayers
The more heaven's hosts will hear our call
By purifying our life and our affairs
Prayers sincerely made can lift our pall
The signal difference 'tween us and all the sages
Is their impassioned communion through the ages

## In Accordance with His Plan

Heal the soul that it may be found true
Heal the heart that it may open wide
Bless the soul that it may so imbue
Its fullest God-potential on this side
The omniscient* light of Spirit never fails
Realigning all to its perfection
The fire breath of God, then exhales
So subtle, it's beyond our frail detection
But for all who hunger for His way
Feel His breeze of wholeness in their soul
Abundant faith and clarity that won't stray
Filigree words of truth on their life scroll
All is made in accordance with His plan
As all is healed and blessed in the world of man

### In Thy Light

By loving what is pure and right
O Lord, may I never pine*
May all I do so please Thy sight
And by Your grace take on a shine
Please take what's less than You from me
Life's joy's becoming more like Thee

Your path of sweetness does enclose
Igniting the boundless light of bliss
Thy love's fragrance is as a rose
A bridge across our life's abyss
Your wisdom pure, my soul takes flight
May I fore'er bask in Thy light

### Inner Calling

We're all here as a touchstone for God's truth
We each have something special to impart
The joy within the soul becomes life's proof
Our calling is directly from God's heart
Where's our place within the scheme of things?
How do we apply our conscious effort?
Self-absorbed or set for what life brings?
Where to turn to when we need support?
Our gift to life need not be thought of great
No one else knows just why our soul is here
Our deepest feelings are not for debate
Fulfillment may not be what it appears
Within our heart we know what we must do
To that inner calling, thus be true

### Joy

God's joy is like a melody
Brought forth from angels' lyre
Quickens the inner eye to see
Beauty, where none was prior

God's joy is like a beacon
Brought down by humble prayer
Abounds throughout and surrounds each soul
A blessing everywhere

God's joy is like a fortress
No dissonance ever found there
Whatever each day may bring us
Won't lead one to despair

God's joy is like a harbor
A peace through all life's tempests
The calm amid life's struggles
Pursuing life's true quest

God's joy, to all apparent
An aura of blessed purity
No place for discontent
It's spun by God-decree

### Joyous Surrender

Receive His jewel upon the wave of being
Each moment pulsing to the plan of God
Not lukewarm as we foster inner seeing
Awaken to the way the saints have trod
We each can be a benchmark cast in light
An example for the ages now today
What we say and do is never finite
Our example set forever on display
To make a change right now, right where we are
This nascent state is what we will perceive
As we're growing strong we'll raise the bar
We'll be amazed with what we can achieve
Joyous surrender is God's way sublime
While leaving footprints in the sands of time

### The Key to Heaven's Door

O blessed light and love of God so true
Help me shape and mold
Restore my faith anew
In Thy time reveal to me
A quickened view that I may see
Serving life, loving, stout and bold

By Thy grace and mercy I'll become
More like You each day
The blessing and the sum
Of everything I was before
Before I closed Your open door
May I by my faith no more delay

A deep abiding peace within I've found
Ever softening love
Less and less earthbound
Inner doors are opened wide
Your blessed truth does help and guide
By Thy blazing fire from above

Test me God that I may humbly be
A beacon for Thy truth
That other souls may see
The path that everyone may walk
A path that's real, not abstract talk
As their life becomes the living proof

As each soul finds harmony and rhyme
Your matrix to fulfill
Blessed and sublime
Every moment so unique
The higher way that all should seek
To truly grasp the meaning of free will

Take each and every mortal by the heart
Make quick their inner eye
Thy higher way impart
By Thy law now let them see
Their life's esteemed by God-decree
No longer need they wander and deny

Fulfilling karmic* law makes all things right
A little bit each day
Transmuting human blight
Everyone's responsible for
Applying the key to heaven's door
And the laws of life, with love obey

## Last Encore

Glorious Father, I beckon thee
Open the portal of my soul
Gracious presence, I do decree
Quicken awareness of my role

Inspire me, blessed Father dear
Kindle now the inner flame
Help me see with vision clear
Your will and mine are now the same

Expand my sense of what is 'me'
As I realize more of You
Hear my fervent, heartfelt plea
As I take in Your celestial view

Becoming whole, a steadfast son
Confusion's bound and held no more
May I serve till my time's done
In what I hope's my last encore

## The Laws of Life

Bind all superiority, that point of pride
A human pride that never serves one well
A conceit that puts our not-self in full stride
Imprisoning the spirit in a mortal shell
A vulnerable breach made in our cosmic aegis*
The weakest link in our ascension chain
A stain upon the soul that's most egregious
The source of all our self-made sin and pain
Pride's the veil that hides God from our sight
The dark star in our limited mortal space
God's sun center's been eclipsed in spite
Of all the human egos' frills and lace
In time the laws of life make all submit
These laws we cannot portion or omit


## Let Goodness Sound Throughout

No one will ever appear inferior to us
When the heart is kindled with sweet kindness
As eyes are opened to a truer vision
One then becomes immune to spiritual blindness

In this life we're servants of each other
And equal in the eyes of God so pure
We'll always be in need of others' service
We all play many roles, be most assured

Look not with scorn on those we think beneath us
It's also done to God whose flame's within them
The humble and the pure see life's best side
No axe to grind or reason to condemn

All we meet deserve respect and dignity
A gracious mien* depicts the higher way
Let goodness sound throughout from soul to soul
The love of God is what we should convey

## Let it Grow

The more we think our soul's within our skin
The less we know of truth, the more of sin
The more we see division all around
The less we sense God's love that does abound
For as we circle the wagons of our mind
Seeing other's souls then as apart
The more it can be said we're truly blind
The less we sense God's single beating heart
This love that's most divine is from one source
Ignoring this does lead to one's remorse
A soul aligned with heaven knows its course
The light of God becomes its potent force
Truth divine resolves all inner woe
The seed is planted, now just let it grow


## Life Lived Sans Regret

Spirit glorious
Sacred presence
Heart of God so true
By our search
And heartfelt longing
May we then find You

Precious heart
Sacred principle
Revealed through purest love
True respect
Hallowed joy
Encouraged by Thy dove

A peace felt undiminished
Thy way shown straight and true
The language of the angels
Their words we shall imbue

Geometric beauty
Found raised in I AM* light
Holy trinity sounded
By His wisdom, love and might

The way is love
The voice is true
His sun shall never set
The blessing of
His presence clear
A life lived sans regret

## Light's Pure Attire

Divinity has a rhyme and rhythm
That keeps its state unseen
The magic hand of purity's way
Sealed to those unclean

A perfected state unfolds upon
Whose heart is in God's hand
This state of bliss concealed until
The time He does command

We draw upon this ray of light
Whose glory's 'yond our realm
It realigns confusion's past
As purity takes the helm

Then all we think, say and do
Is ennobled by His peace
Divinity expands, according to
The faults we do release

Discharge into the Sacred Fire
Our burdens and our ill
Put on light's pure attire
Eternality to instill

## Look No Farther

We're always building walls within our mind
And what they do is subtly shut God out
Except for on His day we're not inclined
When we're busy, it's a spiritual drought
But we amount to nothing without God
Our lesser gods can never fit the bill
God can see the truth in our façade
But He will acquiesce to our free will
There's nothing else in life to ever lean on
Or anyone as dependable as our Lord
What else is there that we could be as keen on?
Nothing else in life is as concord
Look no farther than within the heart
God waits there with blessings to impart


## Lord of Love

The Lord of Love
Came down from above
To help all souls that work
His blessings shown
In the fruit they'd grown
And in service that others shirk

## Love Will Lead to Mastery

Love's written with the finger of the soul
The supernal tracing of a humble heart
Hung 'tween earth and heaven to extol
With eternal beauty to impart
Love's the mighty taproot of our tree
Spreading outward endless, far and wide
The source of beauty in life's buds and leaves
Within this beauty we shall all abide
As love's diffused in all we say and do
It cleanses goals, the rudders of our being
Guides us when life's tests put us askew
To wisdom's flame, the portal of true seeing
Pure love will lead to mastery of the self
A treasure found beyond all earthly wealth

## Make Your Good Indelible

All service in one's life becomes the core
Of the fruitful way
Ascension's 'fuel' to store
Be the mold that all may see
What in truth we all can be
Let God's ideals be humbly on display

Our search for truth is really just the start
'To know' precedes 'to do'
(Though the smaller part)
Make the most of what we've got
Doubt is just the not-self's* plot
And doubt's what puts vitality askew

We need to take our essence by the horn
Not dally or delay
Accepting others' scorn
Become a beam of love and light
Victories won and won in spite
How many hurdles life might thus array

For hurdles are the means of growing stronger
Stronger day by day
Not cowering any longer
As pressure makes the diamond clear
The same is true to persevere
Make your good indelible on life's clay

### Nourish the Seed Within

Commit yourself to find the glow within
God's pure love enfranchised here below
This ember needs His sacred breath to grow
The present's when to let this love begin
Most have had a glimpse of total peace
Though this pearl is frequently submerged
Human frailty is what then needs be purged
That inner bliss may blossom and increase
Our preconceived notions are the block
To cultivating this pearl of greatest price
The laws of life are flawless and precise
Surrender starts the purging of gridlock
Hold this seed within and watch it grow
See how all without does start to flow

## Open Your Heart

Growth in one's attainment's always relative
Relative to the place from whence it starts
Whatever rung our soul is then upon
It rises by the love that it imparts
Whatever stage we find our self now at
No matter in the greater scheme of things
Our gift to give to life is always present
With all the lumined* blessings service brings
Never compare one's self to any other
We're each unique, for no one's as we are
Where'er we are there's always opportunity
For serving life and magnifying our star
So open the heart and serve life with a smile
We're blessed as we then pass each test and trial

## Our Ally

The more of a contact that is made
The stronger is the tie
By staying away through our free will
Self-mastery it belies

By thinning this thread of holy contact
How easily it is broken
God knows then if our heart of hearts
Is sincere or token

Do right in every situation
His will is good and pure
Loving, wise and balanced strong
When firm, the perfect cure

The joy in all this heavenly flow
It's music of the spheres
Enhances from our very core
Allays all doubts and fears

When fully steeped in holy sacrament
Every moment of the day
We'll see bonds of purity are built upon
Full-commitment, not part way

We'll gain some wisdom then in spite
Of cloudiness in the eye
By leaving no spiritual stone unturned
God-reality's our ally


**Our Inner Sight**

Seek and find the straight and narrow road
The straight and narrow's always the safe way
Those who find this vexing, bear a load
The truth that every soul in time must weigh
Human pride's our grounds to turn away
Searching byways for what's straight ahead
Byways only frustrate and delay
Signs of life we have at times misread
By a humble heart, not human pride
Life's signs and cues will lead one ever on
Each day has special moments to decide
How straight will be the road we walk upon
To seek with all our heart we'll surely find
Our inner sight assures we'll not walk blind

## Our Role on this Playbill

For those who think they once were someone grand
Living a life of impact or of charm
It's better that those thoughts are fully banned
This deception of the soul does perilous harm
Near everyone have just been common folk
Living lives the best that they knew how
Imagining one's a king or queen's a joke
Humility's the altar where you'll never bow
The few who've lived that previous life of import
Build a momentum of light that does awake
They'd never in their contemporary life resort
To boasting, which their rank now would forsake
Silence shows the mantle of attainment
Cast in life as self-imposed refrainment

For boasting's a mortal danger to the soul
A selfish coronation of ones pride
That type of immortality's no true goal
Our lesser self is taking us for a ride
These symptoms of the ego run amok
At times, what every soul has had to deal with
Though others' lives can leave one quite awestruck
Stay off that slippery slope of vanity's myth
Let the good we've done in any life
Be sealed within our sacred 'causal chest'*
Spouting off will rend one with its knife
Diminish the flow of all that's pure and blessed
Whomever we have been, now matters nil
What matters is our role on this playbill

## Path to Arcane Truth

We all have a check-list that determines
The quality and the merit of our day
Only when these factors are then met
Is the hoary head of doubt then kept away
But as each day's events unfold before you
Know they're in the realm of heaven's plan
These tests are something that we should not rue*
They make us stronger that we might expand
For we cannot take in the breadth and scope
Or the vision of life's inner play
Our faith upon His goodness helps us cope
And the joy within will not dismay
Be humble on this path to arcane* truth
God will then provide His living proof


## Perfection is Life's Goal

Blessed glorious heavenly light
Expand within each day
By all of God's power and might
Bless each soul we pray

Radiant love, sacred love
Make us more like you
Holy, pure, sacred dove
Your truth we shall imbue

Wisdom of the Christ so pure
Animate each soul
Illumination, density's cure
Perfection is life's goal

## Practice Sainthood Daily

Practice sainthood daily
Examples pure and true
No coarsened worldly way
But a standard to imbue

Though past saints suffered weakness
Their hearts were in God's place
A noble constancy
Examples to retrace

Truth from every faith
Precedence for every age
With unseen guiding hand
The blessed saint and sage

Uplifting admonition
A reverent, pious mien
Trails of humble glory
Heaven's purified sheen

Lured by similar temptation
But stalwart in God's eye
With each decision rendered
Principles did apply

Citadels of Sacred Fire*
Ablaze throughout their time
This timeless path before us
Humility's paradigm

As confusion ever deepens
We can make our lives sublime
When departing, leave behind us
Pure markers etched in time

## Pure and Sincere Heart

Every soul's a fragment of God's purity
A predetermined increment of the whole
A constant faith becomes that soul's security
As more love each day it does extol
It's said, the light of God will never fail
To place our credence in the Rock of Ages
By devotion, truth and love prevail
A sacred path that totally engages
But doubt will dampen the signal pulse within
Befuddling every sincere seekers mind
Easily swayed by all our worldly spin
Too many souls seem negatively inclined
A pure and sincere heart will lead the way
When God's prompting, we'll not disobey


## Quirks and Pearls

Mastery of one's world and one's self
Occurs when we tap the light within
Bringing down the abundance of God's wealth
Unveiling on all life a beautiful spin
Though chaos is encroaching on our space
It's bound and purged, by God's loving grace

Potential good and evil can be found
Within the very heart and mind of man
We all have different levels left unbound
Which gives a shape and hue to each life's span
Contained within's an urge towards light or dark
In some it's very subtle, in others stark

We all have the gift of sensing traits
Though it seems this shouldn't be the case
Within, we're all potential goats or saints
How much of each is filling inner space?
Our world reflects our inner quirks and pearls
Aligned with what in kind each soul unfurls

## Rays of Hope

Kneel, as the angels do above
Their propriety's* the course of every soul
Expand the heart in Elysian waves of love
A goodness throughout our world we must unroll
To stir this age right to its very core
One at a time is how this victory's won
To all who cry out, vow to not ignore

To their world, be as a radiant sun
Angels mostly serve the Lord within
But by the words and actions of our heart
Symbiosis* will find us more akin
Become a somatic* angel counterpart
Angels have much more than harps and wings
In this world they're rays of hope that sing

## Reawakened Progenitor

Symmetry and balance
Out-picturing God-reality
Developing nascent talents
Shunning all duality

A flow of just perfection
Inflamed within the heart
Upward our trajection
Now's the time to start

Seek and ye shall find
Effort breeds reward
As the soul's aligned
She renews the crystal chord*

Nothing that we do
To serve the light's too much
Christic overview
No personality crutch

Human imagination
Tied to what's unreal
Byways of stagnation
Ignoring the ideal

Unenlightened self-interest
A sorry human cause
The higher way repressed
Enough to give one pause

Unenlightened magnanimity*
Progression on life's path
When combined with anonymity
Lessens one's karmic wrath

Enlightened magnanimity
Progression further still
The human's in proximity
To God's sacred will

Enlightened self-interest
Realized full attainment
All of reality's coalesced
In sanctified ordainment

Without reflects within
Below reflects above
The truth that's found herein
Is based on higher love

Reawakened progenitor*
Of the higher way
Heaven's good ambassador
With wholeness on display

## Renunciation

Renunciation* is the spirit of our Lord
It's the step we take towards our perfection
Surrendering what until this time we'd hoard
Willingness does key the right direction
Forced denial is not renunciation
Whether the act's by custom, faith or law
Its purest source, a heartfelt ideation
Any bitterness shows there's then a flaw
Surrender is an opening of the heart
An expanding of the soul's present sphere
That one begins to see they're not apart
All is not as sundered* as appears
When all renouncing's discharged for the Lord
It's the fuel that sends one heavenward


## Restoration

Purest truth is found in purest silence
For silence pure, is the state of God
This silence is the heart flame of His presence
The melting of our illusory façade
Silence is the sterling clear reflection
Of God's presence in our very soul
It's the sound that has no outer detection
The summit of a non-existent goal
The confusion of existence is portrayed
When inner silence is drowned by outer sound
The unveiling of perfection's then delayed
The symmetry of His wholeness can't be found
Silence mirrors our sanctity found within
Restoring our pure oneness that had been

## Sacred is the Byword

We're 'in-divided' portions of the whole
With all the whole's quality in that piece
Upon our inner parts He does enscroll
What by free will we slowly then decrease
A flame within, gathering of itself
Created as a beautiful work of art
We each expand or deplete that common wealth
By our proximity to His sacred heart
We're standing at the door of comprehension
A keeper of the flame, His flame within
Discolored by our doubt and apprehension
Fear not becoming what you've always been
For sacred is the byword of our God
A life beyond this terrestial façade

## Sacred Mystic Fusion

Are we worthy by Thy grace, O Lord?
To serve Thy holy light
Your perfection to restore
To walk Thy path, glittering true
A signal path of chosen few
Arrayed, in Thy blessed power and might

Heroes of all time, saints and sages
Purified holy way
Triumphant on life's pages
Victories won with love and light
Against all odds, still won in spite
Pure examples that we should portray

Duty is each soul's sacred calling
And to God the outcome
The end of our forestalling
Our life's now in His mighty hands
Support come down from angel bands
Now alight with heaven's precious wisdom

By the compass of the higher self
We fathom our direction
Assessing inner wealth
With less and less condemning thought
And more of what His truth has taught
Shedding the skin of human imperfection

Seek life's opportunities to grow
Sacred mystic fusion
Beautiful inner glow
Human want's a hardened wall
Its needs and wishes trite and small
Cut all ties with temporal illusion

### Sand and Foam

Some lessons on this journey we call life
Are very difficult pills for one to swallow
But if we allow form to guide our way
With a heart sincere it soon shall follow

Disappointments trail the one who longs
For a false and limited human joy
A shadow of its heavenly compliment
The roots of what does frustrate and annoy

For any who have lost what they've been given
Offer once again to give them more
And if one doesn't do what they have said
Forgive, and their trust you will restore

As hard as all these tests will seem to be
Let our voice and actions lead the way
Create the form that purity then will fill
For virtues that are God's will not betray

But as these tests come forthright from on high
Be alert to blessings that will follow
As life does surely slap and we respond
A pure heart won't allow us then to wallow

The saints and sages also suffered tests
Through it all they held their heads up high
The bruises taken brought their own reward
Parting dross from gold that's purified

Being always present in our self
That our Lord may find us ever home
Otherwise we'll surely loose His gifts
Our soul is once again in sand and foam


## Schoolroom of the Mother

The light and presence of God's sacred grace
Fills the heart with hope
The humble mien will know its unique place
To live instead of cope

The magic of His fulgent sacred star
A sign in inner sky
As close as indrawn breath, not afar
To raise and purify

A spirit spark that's filled replete with love
To all a blessing dear
Found more in the heart-flame than above
Will tangibly appear

Our God of life is hallowed and supreme
He seeds the earthly plane
To crystallize the full, intrinsic dream
All sentient life sustain

Awaken all to what is heaven's way
Destiny revealed
The cosmic sun expressed, to each portray
His covenant's then unsealed

When all is one, we'll sound the sacred tone
In this schoolroom of the Mother
As the Golden Rule we each enthrone
Found one with every other


## Secret Chamber

Where the love of God does so abide
There's no love of self or anything
No virtue's graced where charity's not applied
With all the good and joy His way does bring

Thus we journey, clad in garments three
Charity with faith and hope, His raiment pure
Without, no union's made sans God-decree
This vest of truth, to the soul ensure

So pure this flame of Spirit, sought by all
The terrestrial transformations now divine
Conversing with the heavens does enthrall
An inward communication so sublime

The more this word's removed from outer sense
We're limiting what our dweller* comprehends
This enlightenment's at the sentient side's expense
Away from the carnal mind that does offend

Though the not-self* is no partner in this contact
By the soul's repose, it surely knows
It provokes the outer, to distract
Riding our weakest link in desperate throes*

These outward provocations come to naught
By grace, the soul does enter deeper depths
Impenetrable silent Om*, she can't be caught
In this chamber, where God's love is kept

## Seek and Ye Shall Find

We'll never know how strong we are
Until life tests our soul
We'll never know our full potential
Or how to play our role

Those seeming strictures on our path
Clarify our way
Where there's mastery, where there's lack
And where we've gone astray

God's dictum* does unfold each day
Through His blessed covenants
With truth that's bound to pious thought
And the blessings that it grants

Religions set forth: "Do unto others
As they should do unto you"
Its essence graced with symmetry
What all should thus imbue

Opportunities abound with each life test
Probing commitment to this law
With each exchange that life presents
Claim victory, don't withdraw

As we show ourselves approved
The teacher will appear
Not through rigidness, but by love
And reasoning sincere

By never accepting platitudes
To the questions of the soul
We've the power to change our life
To finally take control

Don't be trounced upon by life
"Seek and ye shall find"
"Greater works than these" we'll do
As we become less 'blind'

# Seven Spiritual Centers

Of all the numbers available to our mind
None is more important than number seven
With many hidden mysteries to unwind
Secrets from the very doors of heaven
Seven's not only the number of our days
And of the spiraling musical octave plan
It's the color count in our rainbow rays
All are most important to sentient man
It's also the number of our 'spiritual wheels'
Centers stepping down the pranic* force
These chakras* key within divine ideals
Determining every aspirants vital course
These spiritual energy centers thus align
With the axis of the human spine

Known in the Bible as Ezekiel's wheels
Contained in all the teachings of the East
Hidden behind initiatic seals
Through perversion, this knowledge has decreased
View them as a type of anchor point
Resonators for God's spiritual light
Holy centers for heaven to anoint
Not found in the physical or finite
Ideally bringing forth a pattern held
Within the God-presence of us all
By our proper use to finally meld
Within and -out by heaven's protocol
Beacons of energy to polarize His plan
To make concrete the will of God in man

## Sonic Theology

We worship in the sanctum of creation
Sing a song of life within our heart
Set in motion sonic ideations
The distinctive note, that sets each life apart

We're drawn to everyone we find in consonance
With the life-long note of our creation
This motion is sent forth as karmic* resonance
The song of being, that our journey's spun

The purest melody of our inner voice
Builds in concord with creations past
The note and pulse sent forth is of our choice
Its duration started in life's hourglass

Some lives are sung, as a song of love
As some contort and groan in mournful bane
Composing yet in concert with above
Or with our own distorted human strain

As we enmesh ourselves in our modernity
Ignoring our 'Conductor's' clear baton
Beholding not the spirals of eternity
We know not where our melodies are drawn

The fundamental of our spirit's keynote
Is animated by under- and overtones
Our 'sound' is set by how we then devote
Our soul, as we're earning our capstone

Sound's behind the workings of the universe
More than frivolity, they are life itself
This sea of vibration in which we thus immerse
Creates a spiritual poverty or wealth

God is but the consummate composer
Nature's way is as His purest song
What's pleasing to the soul in nature's splendor
Is God's 'voice', that it does prolong

Creation's music's more sublime and perfect
Than any of our humanly devised art
Going within, our soul will then detect
The gracefulness this 'music' does impart

The 'music of the spheres'* becomes the background
Of all that we perceive as sound and light
Intoned by heavenly choirs and thus crowned
By the fire of heaven's Tripartite*

### Spun in Higher Spheres

Every molecule preaches perfect law
All is in its perfect time and place
Even human consciousness, base and raw
Can never stand apart from heaven's grace
All that ever was or ever will be
Unfolds according to His perfect way
Omnipotent and unerring by His decree
A flow is felt in life if we obey
Spiritually we are symmetrical and congruent
For God Himself has geometrized into form
The present is where consciousness becomes confluent*
Hence, all distortion's not the norm
We're a cloth that's spun in higher spheres
The law of life is just as it appears

### The Stock of Heaven's Vein

Greatness unfolds from humility
Success is born of sacrifice
Wisdom's begotten from silence
Keys to each soul's paradise

Forgive as we're forgiven
The good we would bestrew
All life is born within
Do as you'd want done to you

Be in accord with nature
The mother of all form
The place of great encounters
As truth becomes the norm

Let defeat be turned to victory
A lesson at each turn
All's the fruit of consciousness
In this earth sojourn

Circumstance breeds answers
When measured with love's gauge
Turn within for solutions
Cast on this mortal stage

Live the divine motive
Humble and self-forgetful
For life's dynamic symmetry
Ends what's pain and fretful

Don't live the broken covenant
Of unholy lives
Find peace and understanding
See how life then thrives

Search and you shall find
Find and you shall gain
Gain and you'll become
The stock of heaven's vein

## Straight and True

We each can be thus likened to a nail
We go no deeper than our head allows
Some sit on the surface bent and frail
How deep we go reflects what we avow
When God becomes the 'hammer' in our life
What we'll surrender shows how deep we'll go
Is His presence with us full and rife?
How strong can our 'nail of life' now grow?
For some will drive directly to the heart
Others contort from the hammer's strike
God will get us straight and help us start
The nail and our life are quite alike
Become a nail that's driving to life's core
Straight and true is more than metaphor

## Strive

All that belongs to you, belongs to God
All that belongs to God, belongs to you
One in truth, with His staff and rod
By good works we'll take on heaven's hue
Restoring what was once, is the goal
To purify our drop from heaven's sea
Stoke His radiant fire within our soul
Time to claim our Godly pedigree
Let victory be the course of our events
Enabled by His wisdom deep and pure
We're one, when every erg of self assents
Strive, till our ascension is secure
Become a Christ, then you and God are one
As our inner flame becomes a sun

## To Truly Understand

Direct experience is the only knowing
Words alone will never do the trick
How do you describe a breeze that's blowing?
Or the wonder of holding a tiny chick
Words can only grant their fullest meaning
To the one that's lived that situation
All but the encounter's a form of screening
Not the course of spirit maturation
To truly live and to do it wide awake
Blesses the soul with wisdom's lumined ray
The inner senses digest the full intake
Helping the soul receive the full array
Living's how to understand 'to live'
Giving's how to understand 'to give'

## The Tools We Use

When words become more valued than their content
And ritual supercedes understanding
Literature and mechanics are not the path
And illusions are really all that we're commanding

Tools and techniques, then become the barrier
For truth is the annulment of materials
The dynamics of growth make things obsolete
Attachment becomes worldliness not ethereal

Pedantry* and scholasticism dim
The truth and pure nature of heaven's way
To be in the world but not of the world
To be free but to sacred law obey

Worldly things like books of words and practice
Can be of value to the higher calling
But as fertilizer's a part of nature's growth
Any reverence to them assures our falling

Tools, on our path should prompt the state
Where that discipline's found no longer needed
The overt* is the connection to the real
That sacred flower's bloomed that we have seeded

Characteristics are the key, not shape or form
One learns and grows in every situation
The shaping of our behavior's the pressing need
For every affair, its highest pronunciation

Whoever accords with the conduct of occasion
Reaches the attainment of a realized one
For any higher experience is incommunicable
The cloth of its reality's too fine-spun

Three types who seek the truth can then be found
The first is becoming one with God-reality
Followed by one that's yoked to rules and dogma
And one, by whim indulging in banality

But people look for what they want to find
And never seem to find what's not desired
Our emotion can so blunt our understanding
Fixation on the collateral's* where we're mired

Tools at appropriate times will move us forward
Tilling the field of higher ideation
But those same tools can render spiritual harm
When continued beyond their 'use for' limitation

The Buddha's parable makes the point succinct
Employing the raft to cross the river wide
It soon becomes a hindrance on our journey
By taking it with us up the steep hillside

## Triumphant and Sublime

Cast out inward darkness
Fill thy soul with light
Deny the lie of apartness
Be whole with purer sight

The glory of His creation
Divinely thus imbued
This holy ideation
Sagacious* and astute

The hum of seed inception
All matter so endowed
Cast out all deception
Succumb not to it now

The glory of His perfection
Throughout this matter plane
Moves beyond detection
His love's what does sustain

This germinating vision
Crystalized in form
Exactitude and precision
Is perfection's norm

Cast out all thy darkness
With its paltry works
Austere in all its starkness
And the grace it always shirks

Stand for freedom and light
And love in all its forms
Purging human blight
And the truth that it deforms

"Ye are gods"*, it's said
The mark of prophets bold
The chart of nascent divinity
Etched upon our souls

To live the life we're called to
Selfless in all its forms
Within the Christic milieu*
What the soul would call its norm

Radiate and expand
Such joy-inspired play
We're a part of God's command
So why do we delay?

God's light will never fail
Echoes through the spheres
As truth does thus prevail
It casts out doubts and fears

Light, O glorious light
Raise each then in time
Mold us in God's sight
Triumphant and sublime

## True Gold

To those who make their calls to God each day
He relies upon the fire in the heart
To receive His word with no delay
Purifying the soul, is how to start
Be constant as we show ourselves approved
Respond with love to all our tests each day
By life's lessons we'll find ourselves reproved*
For burdens placed on life we must repay
Just how sincere's the heart that makes the call?
With wisdom becoming attuned with holy will
Can the pace we keep be called a fly or crawl?
There's import in our not just standing still
A stalwart, fiery heart is what it takes
As God divides the true gold from the fakes

## We Are a Flame

Everyone's a flame that God has molded
Cast upon a world in mayic* shroud
We blossom as a morning dawn's unfolded
His wisdom's as a light ray through a cloud
On the cusp of First Cause, struggling through
Within a maze we each alone have started
By God's grace our soul shall rise anew
To wholeness known before the soul departed
There was a time our soul was ever gleaming
Our path bejeweled, and our future bright
The glory of His victory 'round us beaming
A ray dispersed with omnipresent light
God wills the soul return from whence it wandered
Purifying His light that it has squandered

## We're Each the One

To every beloved heart
Who resonates with light
Sharpen the mind with study
Be worthy in His sight

By our diligent effort
Be immersed in the Word
For the purpose of our service
To this may we then gird*

Be a vessel of love
Instruments of the Lord
Bringing forth His melodies
Drawn down our crystal chord*

Speak the word of truth
For the enlightenment of all souls
They'll make the inner bonding
To realize their life goals

Be the fullness of Alpha spirit
With Omega understanding
For by this inner change
God's will is now commanding

This conversion comes forth through us
In every level and form
The Holy Spirit will guide us
As we redefine our norm

A momentum built of light
A forcefield of devotion
The dawning of a new age
We each help set in motion

Bind all pride and selfishness
Ambition and all lust
Become a pillar of truth
In whom all may then trust

His light is found within
Allow it to thus emanate
No more fear and trembling
Our path's now pure and straight

Work while you have the light
This mantle's tried and true
Our life becomes a focus
To change the worldly view

Collaborate with heaven
With the hierarchy of light
Friends eternal are they
Our victory to help us write

Part the veil of darkness
Flood your world with light
Be the keeper of the flame
And stand up for what's right

Limitless is potential
When in God we trust
The flow of pure attunement
Sets forth the cosmic thrust

Each one of us can do it
No one can take our place
His light is all around
Filling our auric* space

Expand those radiant waves
Resounding through all time
Such a glorious service
Loving and sublime

Sense the glory of God
And the truth that He has spun
This is the time and place
And we're each the one


## What We've Spun

All that's on the outer is reflection
Reflections of the internal realm of God
All that's known to outer sense detection
Is a part of a delusory façade
Be not bound to sound and form displayed
Its nature's hidden from the outer sense
A misty form of illusion is what's portrayed
And this is done at wisdom's great expense
Hot, sweet, soft, hard or cold
Terms to describe sensorial illusion
They're all inter-dimensional and manifold
Nothing's sensed in insular* seclusion
We with every worldly effect are one
Effects are 'things' that we ourselves have spun

# What Will We Impart?

In love may we desire
To truth fore'er aspire
Uncoil thy burdened soul
From rebellion and resentment
And complacent flesh contentment
For God's the only goal

Mankind would betray
Ignore and disobey
The promptings of our God
Accepting a mean* that's far too low
Serenity and peace we would forgo
Maintaining our façade

By saying all is well
Our debts we'll not expell
We reap what we have sown
No way around God's karmic* law
Sweeping it under the rug's the flaw
As all reality's shown

We each can take the reins
Expel our burdens and pains
And walk a path of light
Blessing all throughout each day
The truth of God we can convey
Standing for what's right

The choice, fore'er our own
We each can set the tone
To shape and mold our day
Building beautiful realms of light
Or selfish, tawdry dens of spite
Which will we portray?

Take time to reassess
If we curse or bless
Try starting in the heart
Pulsing bitter or pulsing love
Carping serpent or peaceful dove
What will we impart?


## What's at Stake

The ordeals that we bear
That sometimes seem as thorns
Can in an instant change
To roses that adorn

It's how the mind has framed
The vicissitudes* of life
In and out of context
Sublime or paths of strife

In truth, all is good
It's lessons for the soul
This schoolroom we call life
Is not our final goal

Prompts can be most subtle
When the eye is clear
The path is quite illumined
Are things as they appear?

Do not neglect these cues
For danger lurks indeed
When ignoring our inner voice
Life's an untamed steed

If attention's placed without
Not on this voice within
Then there's hell to pay
To our soul's chagrin

For God's the coach supreme
Enlightenment the way
The rules are cast in truth
Press on and not delay

Ignore our lessons now
There's adversity ahead
No amount of ignorance
Changes what's foresaid

Life's laws are changeless
Before all time began
There's no exceptions made
Be free in this lifespan

For all we've done is known
There's no hiding things away
We are each responsible
His truth we can't betray

Let conscience be our guide
Humility the road we take
Choose wisely and sincerely
Our ascension's what's at stake

## What's Best for Man

God is light, God is love, God is peace
All that's joy, all that's true, He shall increase
What seems right within the heart is worthy then
As a symbol and a guide for worthy men

What is silent, what is hallowed, what is pure
Becomes a ray of love to thus affect the cure
What is God is good and always so profound
In the beginning was the Word as silent sound

We're each a point of power, wisdom and of love
A unique spark of purest wholeness from above
We traverse this path to truth at different speeds
Depending on the virtue of our works and deeds

By His pure and sacred gift we have potential
By His will and grace we choose then what's essential
With gratitude of heart first sense His mighty plan
Stay humble, for God alone does know what's best for man

## When Making a Call

Mastery's how our personal ascension's won
Not by giving outer factors import
Instead of assigning all to Heaven's Son
Human energies are where we now consort
By cosmic law, God won't intercede
Till we ourselves petition with our call
But karmic* debt and laws will still impede
Delaying God from giving us His all
Know that every call compels an answer
When aligned, we'll realize more effect
But doubt and lack of faith are as a cancer
No truth is gained by human intellect
When making any tender* in God's name
Ask if His and your will are the same

## Where Our Dial is Set

When messages from heavens realm go forth
Those who are attuned will thus perceive
For consciousness is as a radio dial
When we're aligned we truly do believe
When messages of darkness are sent forth
Those that are attuned will thus perceive
For consciousness is as a radio dial
If we become aligned they will deceive
Who's our inner self in amity* with?
Interchange occurs from all directions
The frequency in which our self resides
Is the fount of all our sense reflections
Who we are is where our dial is set
Where it's set is what we then beget


## The Words We Say

God cares little for the place we pray
He's not impressed by rules for meditation
He stays unmoved by idle recitation
Or by empty eloquent words we say

His concern is for the feelings in the heart
Heard through deep-felt praying and decree
Through these He hears our soul's deepest plea
What, in truth, no mere words could impart

He knows when we sincerely call to Him
And fervently mean exactly what we say
He'll answer the engaged heart when we pray
To fill us with His love right to the brim

## Yearn for God

Yearn for God with intensity
He will come to you
Lukewarm is our propensity
Except the chosen few

God and His angel corps
Neglected for a fly
The creaking of a door
Or what we forgot to buy

His truth is not obtained
Or upheld by rote
Our efforts are thus strained
In the coarseness we emote

For wisdom's flame is kept
Through one's life experience
Such a timeless precept
And purest common sense

Still the soul with patience
He's responding to your call
If summoned with a pure intent
His answer will enthrall

On no account abandon
The dream within the heart
As each becomes the Son
His flame He will impart

Seek out our image in
The spirit, not mortal clay
For when we're found akin
Our burdens He'll allay

Our body form is compost
The heart a blooming garden
By tilling to the utmost
All heaven says "Amen"

# 2

# Health & Wholeness

## A Bold Stride of Faith

So pure of heart, at peace and self-possessed
To some, but a dream and not a goal
In our heart of hearts we've all confessed
We'd love to find a way to be more whole
For many have their torment and addiction
Their sphere of being implodes upon itself
The soul is pained without a firm conviction
To search and find that point of inner wealth
Faith, when coupled with determination
In this house of mirrors where we dwell
Gives our God some solid indication
We've had enough self-inflicted hell
The path to wholeness needs a starting step
A bold stride of faith where we once crept

## Achieve a Consummate Life

What we cognize early we retain
To help or hurt our budding inner growth
These habits give a life of joy or pain
But very seldom will they give us both
Such is the state of life, that none feel joy
But by the prospect of an inner change
We're shaped by things that please us or annoy
Though most can't see their spirit's breadth and range
All habits of awareness hurt or grow
We each desire what we think we need
By centering within, we'd all foreknow
Achieve a consummate life with all God-speed
In time all sacred truth is thus believed
As love and will become more interweaved

## All is Well

Discern the light emitting from the soul
Rising through a humble, noble heart
Resulting in a mouth that spreads apart
Let the gift of smiling be our goal
In this light, bouquets are apt to grow
In spite of all of life's supposed wrongs
Through all of limitation's cloudy songs
Let goodness be the sun that we bestow
For what's behind creation is our God
Who is just and perfect without fault
This truth within our hearts we must exalt
As we become His loving, radiant prod
For joy's the clearest signal all is well
Become God's ever-cheerful immortelle*

## Ally or Foe

Lightness in our diet sets a tone
Receptive, open and in full accord
But using food to dull what we bemoan
Is a habit that our soul can ill afford
The more eaten, the denser we become
Excess variety or volume's a burdensome weight
This bulk on inner senses does benumb
Deadening our innate gift to co-create
Body type and effort dictate need
And one cannot go wrong with whole and pure
By exceeding these basic terms we then impede
Most of our afflictions' natural cure
Food can be an ally or a foe
A vital source of wholeness or of woe

## An Enlightened New World View

By raising the limits of what we each can do
Outpicturing the truth that God has placed within
Not simply holding to society's tried and true
For that in fact's what truly is called sin
Attaining full potential's rarely seen
The fear of failure haunts our every move
Too many opt for fantasy or dream
It's safer when there's nothing they need prove
By casting limitations to the wind
We set our sails for destiny's distant shore
"I can't" becomes the verbiage we rescind
Life's now surging from our very core
The pioneer spirit's the life we must imbue
To help create an enlightened new world view

## Appentency

Our approach to diet affects our spirituality
Moving us closer or farther from God's love
Perception's swayed by quantity and quality
To many, thoughts like these are quite unheard of
Hunger, self-imposed, can be quite healing
If that one's devout and so inclined
For then, sensate hunger's quite revealing
To clarify and make things more defined
Appentency* reflects the subtle urge
When pure, this force will flower from the etheric
The corporeal and the incorporeal seem to merge
Don't imagine these concepts just chimeric*
For all that's empty has a chance to resonate
Controlling hunger can help our soul to elevate

# The Art of Living

There's never a reason to lose our temper
At anyone or anything
For harmony is the lube of life
Smoothes the way to God's wellspring

Trying people and trying times
Test the mettle of our soul
When aggravations no longer faze us
We're moving closer to our goal

God will test and test our soul
To be quite sure without a doubt
That we truly are sincere
Committed to go the entire route

For those paying no attention
To their daily dose of bane
Their life is rounds of repetition
Different day, same old same

Until we slowly start to wake up
To sense the method in the madness
We're banged about as a ping-pong ball
With a dose of puzzled sadness

How else then can we thus awaken
To the way things should be done
Without life's rasping* situations
To know what's right and what to shun

By listening to the voice within
Not yielding to each desire's call
Our road of life will even out
No longer just a free-for-all

There's an inner rhyme and reason
For every test that comes our way
The state of mind that we are in
Found on track or gone astray

The art of living starts each day
With heartfelt calls for God to show
How that day's events outplay
To truly help our soul to grow

Then trust in Him as events unfold
They're all a lesson we must learn
Harsh or mild, big or small
Right decisions will be eterne

## The Art of Macrobiotics

It's said, man's god is in his belly
The tyrant that it be
So much time and energy's drained
Climbing that withered tree

This natural function sustaining life
Corrupted beyond compare
Our sense of proportion is slowly lost
In gastronomic fare

The amount and quality have been confused
Amidst our plenteous urges
Nutritional science says this and that
Amidst our diets and splurges

Our higher attunement's thus surrendered
For the reasoning mind
By raising wont* and superstition
Our health can't be sublime

Food plays a part in places it shouldn't
In our emotions and pace of our day
A plethora of ads and faddish gimmicks
Now in our diets hold sway

Where does it end, this worshiping of food?
Of life now so a part
When will wholeness and balanced health
Be the horse that pulls life's cart?

We each decide to open our mouth
And put in what we feel we need
But is this need, real or imagined
So easy for one to misread

Our hunger gauge is blurred or imagined
Buried in habits and woe
To rediscover a wholeness and serenity
We must awaken and grow

Then we'll discover the proper food
Sort the urge from the need
By sculpting a diet based on who we are
We're replanting that illumined seed

For we as humans are integral parts
Of life and the cosmos we know
But narcissism has pulled us away
Stunted our ability to grow

A holistic approach to diet and life
Isn't weird or exotic
But the ancient teaching, "Know thyself"
It's the art of Macrobiotics*

## At One

Simple joy's what gives our life its spin
With hope and acceptance ever balanced true
Life's prospects then become win-win
A lasting drive of good that does accrue
Joy is only found when one's at peace
With every situation and every soul
However you color life does then increase
Make sure the color used is to extol
A joyous heart will not be colorblind
With a cloudy head sunk in the sand
It's rather taking on the Christic mind
For love dissolves the negative, strand by strand
Joy's an inner path becoming whole
At one, with our place and with our role

## Attitude

As we arise to strike a brand new day
We carry over bygones, gripes and bane
How then, in heaven's name, can we portray
Love and truth, on this earthly plane
Holding a grudge towards anyone or thing
Trembles the delicate waters of the soul
A contaminating stench is what it brings
And tainting entries made on heaven's scroll
But gratitude combined with inner joy
As the base for how we start each day
Life's issues seem to less and less annoy
All our gripes and burdens seem allayed
Take a notice of how each day begins
Our attitude will say which way it spins

## Balance

To balance and refine
One needs to combine
Present goals with the past
The higher mind
Aligns the trine
Before the future is cast

The now gives capacity
When mixed with tenacity
As experience provides its wisdom
This insight gleaned
With power convened
Reaps love, truth's purest outcome

## Bastion of Silence

To sense the delicate vision of one's purpose
Glimmering through our daily maze
Immortal light breathes and truly glistens
Within each tender heart ablaze

Embracing love, seed of one's eternity
The fiat of a soul embraced
Master life with all its circumstances
Our innerscape of truth retraced

To unfold, becoming who we are
Be the One that we should be
Hear the whisper of the clarion call
Perfecting love by God-decree

Divine purpose, the heart of all of life
The rhythm of a soundscape true
The hallowed thought within life's sacred verse
This bastion of silence will renew


## Be

Be a cup of rain for those who thirst
A laden tree of fruit for hunger pangs
The parched terrain's sudden full cloudburst
Become what's Yin* to all life's many Yangs*

A room filled with warming, sunlit rays
When any other's house is chilled to bone
As spirits lift on sight of spring bouquets
Or the scent of a lawn that's freshly mown

Be as cooling balm on skin afire
Or as the soothing sounds of a violin
Encouraging words to all who so aspire
The Yang thus realigning all that's Yin

Each and every moment of every day
Life will give to us a chance to serve
Practiced out of love, not as display
It's service that's beyond life's social curve

## Be Flexible

Be flexible but 'pinned'
As a tree in the wind
With its trunk anchored firmly in sod
It's best to be limber
Not rigid like timber
As long as you're anchored in God

## Be Like Water

Water benefits all of life
Unassuming and quite stealth
Satiates thirst that all may grow
A benefit to our health

So practical and adaptable
To each and every shape
Cup, jug, river, lake
Or the grand seascape

Never seeking the mountain tops
No attention for it spun
Always seeking the lowest level
Transformed then by the sun

So give to life as water does
A benevolence to all
Transforming all that we would touch
A cosmic waterfall

## Be Silent

All talk is cheap
A platitude, yes
Live your dreams
Advice at its best

Too much talking
Depletes one's energy
Diffuses our focus
To think and not be

Silence is golden
A platitude, yes
It coalesces energy
Easier to access

Vital forces dispersed
Right through our mouth
They're lost forever
As focus heads south

This wisdom of the ages
That's heaven-sent
Is to know, to dare
To do and be silent

## Become God-Potential

Become the fullness of God-potential
An example for all to see
An inheritance based in cosmic light
Found 'neath the Bodhi Tree*

Let the fire within the eye
And the magnanimous heart
Become the openness of our giving
God's mercy's what we'll impart

Whate'er our self-serving projects are
Those schemes to make us rich
They divert our soul this way and that
Containing one major glitch

The time we spend on earth is numbered
As the hairs upon our head
We must take advantage of our opportunity
We can't help once we're dead

The way so many approach their life
You'd think they had thousands of years
Time to wallow and time to goof off
Living in their close-knit sphere

But our time's a precious commodity
Though an illusion, facts be known
It's still the sea in which we swim
What pearls have we thus sown?

Grab the bull of life by the horns
Be all that we can be
Are we as vital as a river of love
Or a self-absorbed Dead Sea?

As the moth flutters about the flame
It takes but never gives
Are we close enough to warm our niche?
To sustain but never live

For dabbling in God's cosmic fire
Heating the cave in which we dwell
We'll be burned before too long
Stuck in our private hell

For God's an all-consuming fire
A magnet that draws us in
At times we seem to shrug Him off
Blinded by guilt and sin

It's time we find the ultimate joy
Loving service is sweet
The doors are open, let them in
Our heart is their retreat

The more we become a modern example
Of the Buddha and the Christ
The more this light will magnetize
God-Perfection so concise

Study the lives of all the saints
The path each one has walked
They took a stand when needed most
From challenge they never balked

We're each the one who's time has come
Whether living East or West
Live a life that's exemplified
By the saints whom God has blessed


**Become**

All assumed piety matters not
Actions alone can be the only scale
Only knowing, hides the soul's blind spot
Creating a tainted ego-centered tale
Those not living by the words they speak
Have the hypocrite's crown upon their head
Their truth and piety comes up lame and weak
For they will never live what they have said
Physical action has a special dimension
One that shapes and benefits the soul
Right actions pave the road to the ascension
In truth, with life, there is no other goal
Ennobled action is a hallowed fire
Become, and to cosmic truth aspire

## Becoming Centered

Know, then, that focus is the key
Pinpoint attunement with the One
Focusing in the present's how we See
And how we glean the virtues of His son
Wherever and whenever awareness wanders
We're boring into a perfect matrix whole
If one would take a moment and just ponder
Living in the now must be our goal
Unrest, with our current situation
Has the mind wandering near and far
Surrendering to His will's our vindication
And the birthing of a nascent* avatar*
Our point of power's always in the now
Becoming centered is when we start the how


## Begin with Love and Grace

Repetition's a science
And numbers are the key
Sets in motion forces
The flowers of our tree

By engaging our higher mind
To ensoul our very voice
There's worlds to inaugurate
To all of life rejoice

All geometric patterns
Are matrices of light
Coalesced in the physical
Revealed by inner sight

The importance of all numbers
In repetition and in time
Is the science of the ages
Profound and most sublime

The key to its full access
Can be found within the soul
Most use it mindlessly
Not conscious of their role

The structure of our consciousness
Is based in numbers' realm
More than just the clock's hands
We're all completely whelmed

It's the basis of our existence
The dimensions of our space
For what's without's within
Ties hidden without a trace

The beauty of numbers and music
Has its hidden source
Made physical through vibration
Endows our very course

We're a just component
In this sea of creation sound
As the radius and circumference
Are to the circle round

Dimensions are vibrations
Encompassing all we see
Their range is what determines
The ebb and flow of chi

Repetition can be unconscious
As our heart and breath do show
Or as in awakened souls
Their attunement lets them know

By accelerating consciousness
Of atoms and our cells
We become a hub of symmetry
To make heavens and not hells

The only way we'll realize
A peaceful, loving realm
Is to accelerate our vibration
With the Christ mind at the helm

The way to start to access
This higher mind of God
This vibration animating all
Even our earthly sod

Is start to fully realize
The perfection of God's plan
Through divine osmosis
We'll live as purified man

As above, so below
Is the essence of this art
Become what God endowed
The love He would impart

Cycles, seasons, time
All aspects of His mind
Synchro-magnetism
We're connected and aligned

Duality is a distortion
Of the pulse of God's pure rhyme
An asymmetrical vibration
Marring our space and time

All fear and human questioning
Create patterns misaligned
Along with tainted desires
They're what stunt and bind

This all goes back to vibration
The music of cosmic spheres
Repetitions based in numbers
Is how this all coheres

To start to bring to earth
These concepts so profound
Know all music thus defines
These theories turned to sound

With attention to the sounds
We immerse our consciousness in
The people and thoughts we keep
To what our soul's akin

Instead of passing time
And occupying space
Engage in higher qualities
And begin with love and grace


**Blur the Lines**

The call compels the answer's what we're told
So why at times, does it seem not so?
The answer's expressed in what we've each ensouled
But human density's blocking heaven's flow
This human creation is hanging as a veil
A fog that always filters heaven's light
To extricate our self, not just bewail
Illumine with God's love the soul's dark night
We're more than just some idle ideation
Subject to the corruption of the flesh
Swallow not the world of vain creation
To blur the lines is how the soul's enmeshed
By purifying the crystal of the self
We'll help to summon God's eternal wealth

Easier said than done, so what's it take?
This purifying the self seems idle talk
Our day's completely full for heaven's sake
And from a strict regimen most would balk
How far each soul has wandered says a lot
Of what we need to do to get things right
Our free will has ordained what we've begot
Life's path requires illumined inner sight
Every journey's started by a step
Small adjustments accruing over time
Sincere desire's always the best prep
Starting's the hardest aspect of the climb
When God can see the desire in our heart
Then by all His law allows, He will impart

It's comforting to the soul, when it knows
God's mandates are the same for each and all
The more each soul does know the more it grows
Far better than the mortal screech and crawl
By disengaging from the carnal mind
And seeking options to the common way
Opening our heart to God we'll surely find
We're slowly disentangling from life's fray
Know that God alone's our truest friend
All else in life must take a lesser seat
If He's placed first, we find the perfect blend
Tares are parted from life's wholesome wheat
Becoming more like God's the golden key
Start to blur the lines 'tween you and He

## Bottomless Pit

The state of being desireless is a blessing
It's a place of wholeness and serenity
If we resolve within we're not repressing
Cupidity* ties us to our false identity
There's no bottom known to human desire
Its images are ephemeral at best
The urge's sating is no pacifier
Our indulging simply means that we've regressed
Desirelessness isn't acting like a stone
Being inert and lifeless in a chair
But denying the bottomless pit of bemoan
The basis of our self-imposed nightmare
As human desires slowly fade away
Our Higher Self will start to have more sway


## Breakthroughs

When at the door of higher comprehension
Initiations establish where we stand
God will test us in this earth dimension
These tests are universal to all man
Trouble many times will lead to woe
But tests can be a period of instruction
Giving up's a self-imposed plateau
For one's inner growth, the worst obstruction
All have what it takes to change trajectory
To turn within and hear His inner voice
He'll provide the wisdom and direction
With love and power to implement His choice
Breakthroughs once again bring forth the dawn
Of greater illumination and progress drawn

# By Trust

No cycles are ever triggered
By any time or date
These rhythms are internal
No schedule can subjugate

It's a trusting in our self
And what God has planned for us
Attuned to inner workings
Surrendering to His trust

But with any doubt or fear
We block this inner flow
It's a sign we just don't trust
God knows how we must grow

Surrender is a principle
The bane of human desire
But it's an integral part
To accelerate ever higher

Inner peace becomes the clue
His path we'll then adore
Let the structure of particulars
Out-picture from our core

By trust, His way's found true
When aligned He will compel
Our soul to rise up higher
From out this mortal cell

## Celestial Star

The one who makes a sacrifice
So another may succeed
Can be called a true disciple
To serve's life's purest creed

By surrendering to the calling
With sacrifice and love
We're accruing sacred treasures
In our heaven found above

For sacrifice, when joyous
Is what life's all about
Helping others and our self
Blessings gained without a doubt

Do unto others is the teaching
From every faith and land
Spreading love throughout our life
An example for all man

All effort done with love
Consecrated in God's name
Assures that one of grace,
True honor, not worldly fame

Success cannot be weighed
By fortune or worldly pride
For all good works we do
Starts waves of love world-wide

We each must play our part
And change right where we are
Compassion, love and charity
Brightens our celestial star

## Charge the Soul

To make each cycle fresh and flowing forth
Takes the slightest turning of our 'dial'
Variety keeps our needle pointed north
Sort of like a disciplined freestyle
Mindless regimentation stifles growth
Slowly has our awareness tuning out
Bored or focused, we never can have both
But a glowing day is dulled by human doubt
Our daily heaven or hell is of our doing
Demanding that each day be turned our way
When flexible in our approach and in our viewing
There's less and less a chance we'll be dismayed
If more serene and productive is the goal
Variation of routine will charge the soul

## Chewing's Nature's Cure

The art of mastication* has been lost
In a voracious sea of gulping it down
It issues out of habit, at a cost
Giving our body's system quite a 'frown'
It's stage one of food's assimilation
But a harried life will lead one to devour
A process learned from kinfolk imitation
Eventually leading to a stomach sour
Chewing fifty to a hundred times
Especially if our food's not whole and pure
Lack of chewing's a gastronomic crime
And lots and lots of chewing, nature's cure
When eating, try to find a settled mind
Better to do the masticating grind

## The Choice is Ours

Repair the roof, when the sun is shining
Not all stressed, in the pouring rain
Times of peace are for the soul's refining
Not jumbled amidst all our stress and pain
Shoring inner ramparts is the goal
To elevate and thus protect the soul

Deal with any weakness right away
A security that will help us ever through
These weak links in our chain will sure dismay
Life then makes our soul so black and blue
Only humility will alert us to the crack
To be aware before that karmic* whack

Don't take for granted any preparation
Pride says, "I'm not worried, I'm immune"
Stalwartness, not part of the equation
Vanity means our soul will not attune
The choice is ours to balance love and power
With wisdom, that the nascent Christ may flower

## Choosing Wisely

A stomach full's a burden to the soul
Dense and heavy drains our light away
It's time that we decide just what's our goal
And know if God-reality will hold sway
Food's purpose is to strengthen and to heal
Eat just enough to soothe the hunger ache
Emotions mean the wrong foods will appeal
Then our eating's not for wholeness sake
Abuse for years has dulled the 'I'm full' gauge
For feeling full is not health's true intent
Food is not the potion to assuage
True desires give pure nourishment
Food's the fuel that powers our soul's horse
By choosing wisely it helps us know our course

## Christ Essence

Our ego is a mountain
Over which we cannot see
It blocks our view, of what is true
With thought, one should agree

This point of pride, we take in stride
Is to our detriment
It does erase, purity's grace
What's whole, it does fragment

The knot it ties, magnifies
All that's smug and vain
Petty issues, constant miscues
God-reality's bane

But the ego has a part to play
In the scheme of things
For a humble heart, will so impart
Peace from daily stings

Humbleness, will so caress
The thorns on our life's way
Our identity, by God decree
Christ essence on display

## The Clock is Not a Rock

There's too much stock
In the hands of the clock
One needn't dismay
If from it we stray

'Cause sunrise and sunset
Midnight and noon
Are points in eternity's
Cosmic loom

Schedules to keep
Obligations in trust
By the timekeeper's pulse
We boom or bust

For time is fluid
Consciousness the key
Our mind controls it
With examples you'll see

In good times the hands fly
In bad times they drag
How can what's exact
Seem to rush and lag?

Our state of mind's
How we sense time
Its flow and its rhythm
'Tween each hour's chime

Just like the space
From point A to B
There's infinite gradations
By heavenly decree

By making attunement
To all that's true
Our consciousness expands
Time opens and renews

Create maximum time
For what needs be done
By surrendering to God
The more victories won

But densify self
With doubt and worry
We'll see once again
All's flurry and scurry

The peace of God's presence
Is where to begin
This rock of the Christ
Is found within

Plant this seed
Nutritious its fruit
Time's now an ally
In mastery's pursuit


## Constancy

Banishing our frustration and dismay
With hope and patience may we carry on
Perseverance is more than just cliché
But one of life's important paragons
Sticking to it breeds its own reward
It's how reality, in time, will bend our way
Experiencing situations in accord
Awareness focused, not in disarray
Constancy earns the spoils of this life
A virtue blest by heaven's holy writ
Victory's opportunities are so rife
A truth attained that's never counterfeit
With it rock is altered by a drip
And we with God develop fellowship

## The Cosmic Laboratory

Heaven's glory opens many doors
A magnificent glory found within the heart
Limitation's what the soul abhors
Let each day become a brand new start
All potential's contained within each moment
All boundaries are then born of doubt and fear
But revelation requires our consent
With a heart that's open and sincere
If we're truly awake it doesn't matter
What we do, for all's then based in love
Our energies focused, not diffused and splattered
The source of all that's truth is found above
If the heart's the door to heaven's glory
Our life becomes the cosmic laboratory

## Do Unto Others

Notice how quickly petulance* turns to ire
Just how quickly we'll flash our tooth and claw
Mortal bane creates our lives' quagmire
The Golden Rule's no longer common law
What's sent out is as a boomerang
Stones we've cast will hurt us on return
Before our words set off a mighty bang
This perfect rule of life can help us learn
We're all one in God's radiant love
Let this teaching be our guiding power
Change your ways upon the receipt hereof
"Do unto others" needs be life's avower*
Know all you've sent to life will thus accrue
And all that you've sent out is done to you

## Doctrine of the Heart

The greatest lie of life is being bored
Desecrating who and where we are
Change things by the Spirit of the Lord
Glory unto glory's pure attar*
Qualify all life with heaven's grace
For every moment's filled with God-potential
Engage in spirals of goodness to retrace
Spreading throughout all life, what's essential
We're then infused slowly with God's Love
As this sun expands its healing ray
This inner revelation's from above
This doctrine of the heart is heaven's way
Let every day be blessed with so much joy
Where're we are, God's love's what to employ

## The Eden Way

To win the heart of God as well as man
Do more than we would desire done for us
Showing loving kindness is God's plan
It's how we each can build a bridge of trust
Duty must be first borne in the mind
We're here for more than seeking carnal pleasure
Self-absorption is the flaw that binds
A barren way for those who seek God's treasure
All virtues bloom, from a sense of being
Not from any vain attention seeking
Weave a life of purest inner seeing
Be a quasar in the heavens streaking
To commit one's spirit to the Eden way
Flowers our sense of reality day by day

## Enlightened Action

Our actions need to culminate in wisdom
As an infant's hand does with a fire
Too many never resolve this great conundrum
Before life's ticking hand does thus expire
Gaining wisdom's a process we control
How open are we to its guiding hand?
Too many aren't accepting of their role
As life's hourglass drops its precious sand
All action in this realm will start a wave
A wave that then resounds right through the spheres
What we say and do will then engrave
We each create our world as it appears
Enlightened action's a tie with wisdom pure
The only way our soul can then mature

## Expend Yourself

Exhausted at day's end can be a blessing
If our efforts past were based in love
For then those weary bones came not from stressing
But rather a sacred alliance with above
Giving all we've got, and with honor
Creates a void that God will surely fill
Though this day has now made us a yawner
We've helped to lower our debit on life's bill
Our days start out so pregnant with potential
It's our responsibility to follow through
Not griping, but with gratitude's essential
To realize full potential, our destine true
Expend yourself in all you do this day
Though wearied, then give thanks to God and pray

## Fast and Pray

Whatever are the burdens of our soul
All we need to do is fast and pray
Then our higher mind will take control
Combined with meditation day to day
For questioning is a major part of living
Sincere petitioning helps to get it right
All the answers that our God is giving
Will guide our soul to someday reunite
Truth will be the shield of victories won
Tapping into Spirit's infinite wealth
A pearl of greatest price is what He's spun
It's something that our souls have all forefelt*
All fasting and all praying's for our soul
They help to bring us closer to life's goal

## Fasting

Abstaining from food
This most dearest thing
Done throughout history
So what does it bring?

Sacrifice comfort
At least at the start
Cleanses the system
Good health to impart

Our body needs rest
Besides each night's sleep
Our organs work hard
Good health won't come cheap

No food in the mouth
The stomach can rest
The first time we try
Temptation's our test

Our appetite wanes
Hold firm to the task
Are benefits gained
Worth it you ask?

Our desire for food
A most basic urge
The root to healing
Gluttony to purge

Toxins reduced
Our cloudy mind clears
Concentration and focus
Better than in years

Neglect and abuse
Our parents didn't know
They were just doing
What their parents sowed

Cleansing the system
Brings forth a rebirth
Not to mention
A much trimmer girth

For light is the 'food'
Of spiritual vision
The body is helped
By our decision

Whenever the belly
Is greedy for food
Not indulging it
Improves attitude

But fasting is more
Than abstaining from food
Skip TV or sweets
A welcome interlude

No spending or talk
No radio blare
We decide how long
But with no fanfare

The way to improve
With energy aligned
There's palpable change
As fasting's redefined

A fast from a habit
Or food of our choice
Opens up vistas
Our soul does rejoice

To break from the 'same old'
Expands inner sight
God's now our 'bread'
Truth more than trite

For excessive desire
Burdens the soul
This bird of paradise
With freedom its goal

## Food That's Whole

We dig our graves with our teeth
With one mouthful at a time
To cover up what's underneath
It speeds our feeling past our prime

Habits gleaned when we were young
When choices poor still left no clue
Now our diet's chain has hung
Our burdened health for our review

Ignorance always takes some time
To fully manifest in our bod's
Slowly starving nerves and mind
But we ignore life's gentle prods

As things do slowly come apart
We still take in the same wrong stuff
Common sense could make us smart
If not so tied to desire's bluff

As soon as a connection's made
Between our food and how we feel
Bad choices will then start to fade
As food that's whole gains more appeal

### The Four S's

We each have a gift
Bestowed from on high
There's no time to dally
As lies pacify

Become artisans of Christ
In our life's endeavor
Through His love and truth
All banal ties sever

We all have talents
Both revealed and unseen
These blessings of God
What our past has gleaned

Capitalize on potential
While the iron's hot
Opportunity is precious
So give it your best shot

And remember the four S's
Naught comes without them
The basis of fulfillment
The keys to life's stratagem

Selflessness and Service
Sacrifice, Surrender
The path to our victory
And unlocking God's splendor

## Frame of Mind

Events perceived en masse, or alone
Were once probabilities unfulfilled
That's why the future is for most unknown
And why some outcomes may not play as billed
With vision ripe, we'll sense the quantum waves
Ere they give way into a clear event
The awareness of the observer's what engraves
All life essence with our soul's consent
How all's perceived varies with each soul
We're all turning potential into reality
When not aligned with the Christ-perfected whole
Life is viewed with schisms and duality
Whatever frame of mind we each are in
Helps create a world of love or sin

## Friend or Foe

Intervals of time in their linear succession
Are measured by our living thought alone
Illusion is the feeling of progression
Unfoldment's simply all that we have sown
For nothing's real, but the eternal now
The present has been called our 'point of power'
By opening the single eye* within the brow
Time unfolds then as a cosmic flower
Being illusory, the mind constricts or expands
The very fiber of our sense of time
Our limited state creates life's dropping sands
Creating then a stressed or tranquil clime
Absorb time's measure, as a friend or foe
Dimly lit or vibrantly aglow

## Giving It Your Best Shot

Leave no stone unturned
In faint unconcern
There's victory in giving all you've got
For less than your best
Is lifelong unrest
Don't quit before giving it your best shot


## God or Mammon

Doing is more important than recognition
Serving the will of God's its own reward
Inner glories expand to full fruition
With silent recognition by our Lord
Efforts to gain attention do real harm
Jade the soul to always thirst for more
Others' notice has a worldly charm
We're always rowing but never finding shore
Let no one know the good that we would do
Let others have the glory if need be
The good that's done for God shall all accrue
A force of light made great by God-decree
Decide, now, what master ye shall serve
God or mammon's the capital you'll preserve


## Gratitude

Gratefulness in character
Is as fragrance in a flower
An avowing of our source
The well of grace and power

In whom it's then found lacking
That one's devoid of beauty
Express appreciation
For it's one's sacred duty

The gratitude we express
For every word and deed
The more we'll sense God's presence
Answering every need

The means by which we garner
His mercy poured upon us
The salvation of our soul
When troubled, such a plus

As the sun, rain and earth
Create food we eat
To have no sense of thanksgiving
Makes life incomplete

Acknowledging others' efforts
Develops within our mien
Graciousness in temperament
A beauty so supreme

But as we weigh and measure
What's done for you and me
We waste our time computing
What's set by God-decree

The card in life we're dealt
Is part of life's just scheme
Unfolding in perfect order
Or as a vexing dream

Ingratitude shows one's ignorance
Of the source of all our trials
The result of the Golden Rule
Digging through our karmic* piles

The first lesson of all gratitude
Is forget what we do for others
And only thus remember
The efforts of our 'brothers'

For it's our sorry ego
Demanding life pay heed
Its vanity knows no bounds
Attention, its dire need

The one that knows life's story
From whence all blessings come
By expressing heartfelt gratitude
Moves toward life's victory won

A saying for all times
A blessing that's most fateful*
Is "Life is perfect, I AM* blessed,
Hear O Universe, I AM grateful"


## Healing is by Giving

Taking without giving's 'spirit cancer'
Cannibalism in another sphere
Like the disease ravaging body cells
Though it could be argued, more severe
Receiving just by giving is the law
We're a poison when we're always taking
Our selfishness becomes a fatal flaw
Ignorance is the core of our forsaking
We each are body cells upon this earth
Are we a pathogen* on this corporeal plane?
The elixir and the cure's a soul purgation
Is our energism* lifting or a drain?
Healing is by giving on life's path
Purified by His love, the aftermath

## Healing is Divine

Ponder exactly what good health's about
A miracle as our body mends itself
We slow it then by voicing fear or doubt
It's quickened by our tapping inner wealth
What else in life is blest with self-repair?
Always striving for a matrix whole
Ignorance has become our lifelong dare
Constant abuse and recovery, an unwise goal
But living in accord with innate law
Completeness found beyond the sensate realm
God's presence that's within is where we'll draw
Wholeness to our core, love at the helm
Healing is divine when not delayed
There are no limits when cosmic law's obeyed

## The High Way

Duality's never but a lone event
But a subtle matrix opening wider
On all that's pure and whole a mighty rent
With God's sacred laws, a sure divider
For illusion will beget more of its kind
As a fire destroys all in its path
Its fuel's the deception of the carnal mind
Truth is singed then by its baneful wrath
In time the path of life becomes more sinuous*
Twisted human folly's now the norm
The shadow and mirage become continuous
To God-reality the soul does not conform
Don't confuse the byways with the high way
Or life's oneness as a trite cliché

## How We See Our Self

Purpose is the force that spurs us all
Without it life would seem a muddled ride
Our special mission's sensed through prayer and call
The key's if we and God's will are allied
To sense our cause for being, soothes the soul
Animates every aspect of our being
Just getting by's not living our true role
Life is more askew and not agreeing
To have a vision appearing just and right
The sense that this is why we're really here
It's thus revealed by ripened inner sight
Knowing when to move on or adhere
When how we see our self aligns with God
Our life is based in truth, not some façade

## Humility

The road our soul does travel on
Is for the polishing of the heart
The polish we ought be putting on
Is humility from the start

For humble living will not diminish
But opens up life's door
Realizing this is God's true wish
His wisdom at our core

But true humility cannot be taught
It's the teacher of itself
Daily practice is how it's sought
Not from some bookshelf

This virtue of such vast import
Is difficult to learn
Its precious yield lends much support
To help us thus discern

His grace is through this humble way
Not the way of the proud
These blessings rise to wipe away
Our spirit's densest shroud

Complaints and brags will make it clear
Humility's not one's mien
It's best to hold to silence dear
A presence, most serene

There's joy found in the humble way
A peace is thusly gleaned
Taps the truth of life's bouquet
From pride, the soul is weaned


### Ignorance Never Knows

If all we seek in life is what we know
How in heaven's name can we then grow?
To fully grasp ideas that are brand new
One needs to know within just what is true
So how can one discern truth from a lie?
What's the standard used to verify?
It's humbly being centered in the heart
To find the truth that all life does impart
By weighing concepts with an open mind
No longer just the blind one following the blind
There'll come a recognition in our soul
Of truth that brings us closer to our goal
No more is added to a mind that's packed
And ignorance never knows what it has lacked

## Inflow Affects Outflow

Too many people's lives
Are governed by their urges
If nothing else survives
There's still their gluttonous splurges

The source of all our woes
Is undisciplined emotion
For whatever's coddled grows
Igniting inner commotion

We're stuck in a vicious round
Putting food in our mouth
Bad things to eat abound
And most will point us south

The Catch-22 we're in
Is caused by the foods we've eaten
They're the ones that begin
Our feeling so browbeaten

Life's problems need attention
Without that plate of food
Better to try abstention
Than inciting a gastro-feud

Eating the proper food
Without the sugar and fat
Starts to improve our attitude
we're much less stressed or flat

Our food's quantity and quality
Affects just how we grow
A consequentiality
How inflow affects outflow

## Inner Command

Many people asleep are still 'awake'
And many awake, in truth seem more 'asleep'
The attunement of the soul is what's at stake
Awareness is set by our karmic* heap
For those awake, sleep's a new vibration
The soul is simply moving by degree
It's much more than a dreamy aberration
Or some virtual-reality fantasy
Then there's those whose day is more a dreamland
Not wide awake to who or where they are
Phantasms mean the body's now unmanned
The day just passes by with mind afar
Inner command is shown with blatant clarity
When what's within and —out has no disparity


## Inner Peace

Allowing others to express their finest aspects
Removes them from the walls of our creation
In confining them, we also stop ourselves
For others see us through this limitation
We're all the fruition of one blessed God
And all are doing the best with what they know
Irregardless of how we think we see each other
Verily, everyone's desire is to grow
For what we see about is what is in us
What's without is truly what's within
The best or worst in life would not be seen
If not for what we now or once had been
May the love and good we see in life increase
It reflects how much we live with inner peace

## Just Deserves

Some pursue their happiness
While others would create it
As some live for the moment
Others loathe to dissipate it

One lives for the ego
Another humbly serves
When each one's time is up
To each his just deserves

## Know the Pulse

Knowing when to stop and when to start
In God's time unveils an inner peace
In truth, it's a most essential part
Of finding flow not whim or vain caprice*
We, by not sensing life's pulsation
Are under- and overdoing many things
Getting wrapped up in our consternation
Absorbing all life's pulls and all its stings
The feeling in our gut will let us know
When it's time to stop or time to move
By going with its prompts we'll start to grow
Discerning the flow of life, we're in the groove
To have a sense of what we should be doing
Know the pulse within is heaven's truing

## Know When to Stop

That chilled chamber of 'horror'
Always tormenting the soul
By eating more and more
Our vitality's what it stole

Seeds, fruits and vegetables
Nuts, beans and grains
Life's most basic staples
When eaten, no drain or pain

But when poor choices are made
With amount or with quality
Our discipline will then fade
In gluttonous solidarity

We're digging our own grave
With the chomping of our teeth
Indulgence does enslave
Disorder's what it bequeaths

What's not liked wont hurt us
Show temperance with what you do
Over-eating's not life's purpose
A most unhealthy brew

Too much gluttony and gourmet
Is never good for the soul
Simplicity is life's gateway
If you long to reach your goal

## Laugh

Enjoy a good laugh
When it is apt
For laughter sooths the soul
Whether humor or gaffe
A yuk-yuk untapped
Relieves stress to make one whole


## Less Sleep

There's a way to thrive on far less sleep
If we so aspire
So much more to reap
Inspired and in total wonder
Each day's whole, not cast asunder
Running on heaven's light that won't expire

In truth, every moment we're renewed
Breathing is the key
Getting energy unglued
Shallow breathing shuts us down
'Cause prana* makes us whole and sound
We simply need to relearn how to breathe

Sleep's affected by the food we eat
Indulging zonks us out
Plus eating too much meat
Plentiful variety's a dangerous brew
And what we eat needs much more chew
We're not fatigued, but feeling hale and stout

Perfection's in the rhythm and the flow
Attention held within
Finding our pace to grow
The course and cadence of our day
No date or clock can e'er display
We're each unique, like no one else that's been

See all experience exactly as it is
Life's a constant lesson
Life's a constant quiz
The higher mind has all solutions
Minus human convolutions
Make the call for heaven's intercession

The more that we're aligned with heaven's will
The more we see our place
No sacred energy spilled
Good momentum does accrue
Become aligned with the cosmic view
With far less time upon our pillowcase


## Life is Perfect

Repeat aplenty
'Fore life unloads
Anything ominous or fateful:
"Life is perfect
I AM* blessed
Hear O Universe, I AM grateful"


## Life's Sum

If we say, "I'm tired"
That's just what we'll be
It's our thoughts and words
That create our life-decree

By saying that we can't
Then we never will
We've now set the tone
A life that's now standstill

Watch what follows "I am"
For that's what you'll become
Along with visualization
Producing our life's sum

## Life's True Mission

Tomorrow dawns a brand new day
A chance to try and try again
To find a more enlightened way
The schisms in our being mend

Our awakening has a glistening start
Not folding the hand that life has dealt
By residing more within the heart
All blocks to joy begin to melt

Discipline based in love's the way
Through an open, purposed aim
The slate is clear to start each day
To slowly raise the 'wholeness' flame

Faith's a power lodged in the heart
Controlling the whole of one's true place
Affirmed each day, the soul's rampart
A blessing felt by God's good grace

May we not through weak resolve
Deny each day its full fruition
When our heart through His evolves
We'll fulfill our life's true mission


## Lighten Up

Self-deprecation
Is healthful for the soul
'Cause those who are so serious
Need levity to be whole

If one is truly humble
They'll laugh at their expense
Loosen the reins and lighten up
Life needn't be so tense

# The Living Proof

Perfect love will cast out doubt and fear
The light of God produces strength within
Our human enigma's not as it appears
Restore perfection, just as it has been
Doubting God and fearing the unknown
The blight of every lesser human self
A limiting matrix that we each have sown
Not tapping into heaven's infinite wealth
The lies of all our modern day illusion
Puts us in a web of such deceit
Our lesser selves revealed are in collusion
Based in human vanity and conceit
The higher self's the way to heaven's truth
Wholeness then becomes the living proof

# Macrobiotic Living

A healthy body molds a healthy mind
The healthy mind will sire poised emotions
Being so aligned is most sublime
It can be done sans taking pills or potions
All one needs are veggies, beans and grains
With a little fruit, nuts and seeds
Helps in healing all our aches and pains
Pure and whole is what our body needs
By eating modern, 'disembodied' food
Either 'healthy' or, off the grocer's shelf
Vibrancy is not what we'll exude
But a waning of our inner and outer health
Macrobiotic* living's its designation
Living in harmony with life, its application

# Mistakes are OK

Those who achieve greatness
Always fail more often
To the ordinary among us
Failure is our coffin

Learning from life's miscues
The path of fortune's devotee
Striving creates more faux pas
In the attainment of true mastery

## Mystic Art

When the soul breathes in a sacred silence
And its body vessel falls away
The grace and beauty of this hallowed calm
Is how it shames the worries of the day
For while the soul's in concord with this silence
It's gone beyond its dense and muddy vesture
Beyond the spikes and spears of daily toil
By the glory of this hallowed gesture
For by this simple act of supplication
An act born of a reverence of the Lord
Becoming realized in this quiet realm
Found, with God's love now in accord
Mystic art of silent meditation
The higher peace of divine exultation

## North or South

The less we use God's light in carnal ways
The less food we're putting in our mouth
The more we'll see this inner discipline pays
The less we'll see our energies heading 'south'
For each of us is granted a small portion
A unique sliver of heaven's infinite love
Do we expand or shrivel in contortion
Determines how we'll use this light above
By His law, right use accrues much more
Blessings human minds can't comprehend
To abuse or hoard the gifts that we have stored
The results we get have only human ends
Open the heart and let His light shine forth
Then we'll find our energies heading 'north'

### Not the Way to Deal with It

When upset, tired or stressed
Stay away from the fridge
To know when enough is enough
Is lost when we cross that bridge

Then food's no longer our friend
Wrong reasons for piling it in
Problems need to be dealt with
Not buried in a plate of Yin*

For proper diet can help us
To see with a clearer eye
Gain control of emotions
Heal and purify

But dealing with our problems
By tossing food in our mouth
Only leads to suppression
And sending our energy south

By going back to basics
To a diet pure and whole
Adjusted for each lifestyle
For balance is the goal

Challenges are better met
With whole food in our gut
Moods and energy flow
Not soaring or in a rut

By living closer to nature
The way it used to be
Food's once again a friend
Try it, I think you'll agree

# Observations

*Gentleness*
Considerate and benign
Disarmer of the fierce
Melter of the stubborn
As the proud bubble's pierced

*Order*
It's nature's way
Heaven's first creed
Our efficiency depends
On organization to proceed

*Life*
A mystery to unravel
Not a problem to solve
It's a wonder to behold
As we grow and evolve

*Tact*
People who use it
Have less to retract
And generally they'll find
No foot to extract

*Backbone*
Creatures without them
Have the hardest shells
Humans without them
Live in self-imposed cells

*Income*
We need to be frugal
Not above our means
We don't need to live
Like kings and queens

*Smiles*
They're only sincere
Depending on whether
The heart and the mouth
Are working together

*Diamonds*
They're nothing more
Than chunks of coal
Made good and pure
Under pressure's toll

*Limits*
Bars to be raised
There to be tested
The finest effort
Can always be bested

*Ignorance*
There's times that everyone
Tends to show some
The subject's the difference
Of who appears dumb

*Idleness*
The refuge for those
Possessed of weak minds
A holiday for the misled
All momentum it binds

Take to heart these thoughts
For truth sets you free
'To know' is good
But it's better 'to be'

## One and the Same

Be careful when we use the spoken word
For God endows our voices with His power
Be not discord's agent provocateur
Instead, become peace and love's avower*
Our voice is like a cosmic thunderbolt
Birthing many worlds on many planes
Agitation's as a mighty jolt
Polluting the world with impure verbal stains
The slightest change of quality in our voice
Actuates vast schemes of change throughout
First controlling anger's the right choice
Becoming aware of what our voice can sprout
It's said I AM's the power of God's name
Know when spoken, that we are one and the same

## One at a Time

In this land of abundance of all food
Why, do we compromise our future?
What starts out whole we process and denude
But natural is our modern culture's cure
"You are what you eat," is more than trite
Our body's made new every seven years
Ignorance and addictions are the blight
Doing much more damage than appears
By desiring our convenience and more speed
Sugar, fat and salt's now in control
It's opposed to life and Nature's sacred creed
And the vibrant future we would all extol
Take the time to learn and then eat right
One at a time we'll help our world unite

## The Only Constant is Change

The only true constant
In our life is change
No matter what the effort
To plan and thus arrange

Surrender like the lily
As it floats upon the rill
Its direction is assured
Yet its place is never still

Going with this flow
Is not thinking through the head
By the pulse of intuition
We'll never be misled

Not floating on some whimsy
Adrift far off the shore
But anchored in the Christ
Our higher mind's at the fore

This inner pulse of truth
Springs forth as wisdom's child
This voice heard from within
Is forthright or quite mild

This purest inner sense
Saying change or carry on
It sees the bigger picture
The course to set upon

Learn to know its voice
From the chatter in our head
Its source is wisdom's loom
Weaving life with cosmic thread

At times it makes no sense
To its prompts stay ever true
As the veil is slowly lifted
It broadens our inner view

Sincerity is the gauge
The proof's contained within
It directs the steps we take
Illumines where we've been

Then away we will go
With Spirit at the helm
Through life's jagged reefs
To the port of heaven's realm

### Opened Door to Wisdom

Most every soul has binding psychic knots
Knots of pain that ever hold them back
Though plain to others are these karmic spots
Many would protect their pain and lack
The periodic recurrence of situations
Where we find we just don't want to deal
Burdened and discordant confrontation
Signs that certain areas need be healed
Many will just pass right from life's screen
Never to confront these self-made blocks
All life's signs and signals go unseen
Chances wasted on their cosmic clock*
We each have blocks we need  to overcome
Before we'll see the opened door to wisdom

### Our Body Showcase

Drink, only when thirsty
Hunger's the reason to eat
For many it's simple and trite
When weighed in their self-conceit

Well, why else would we partake?
Or imbibe our favorite drink?
As we examine our motives
It hopefully will get us to think

The pleasures of wholesome food
Radiate a comfort within
Balances our different energies
Motivates with positive spin

But even too much of a good thing
Burdens as energies are drained
The less we eat, the better
Then our body's not stressed and strained

Our indulging's a force of habit
With ulterior motives at play
It covers what we won't look at
When exposed to the light of day

Our emotional state is displayed
On our girth and face
Pretensions aside, there's nowhere to hide
It's there on our body showcase

## Our Good Deeds

Keep all good deeds silent
For why should anyone know
God's our only confidant
Not anyone here below

Silence is so golden
Especially with the good we do
By tooting our own horn
Good works will go askew

For worldly recognition
Is its just reward
No good momentum gained
And no heavenly accord

Learn to become satisfied
That God knows what we do
No need to puff our sails
And vanity pursue

For all that we keep silent
Builds a cosmic trust
That account's held in heaven
God's law, loving and just


## Our Voice

Most all our debts to life are with our voice
Most conversation leads to levels low
But as in all of life, it's still our choice
How low will we allow our words to go?
Abusing life with many statements vile
Gossip and profanity's second nature
One word can still create a karmic pile
The source is always a consciousness impure
Keep watch on what you say and how you say it
Is what you're saying promoting love or hate?
If not love, it's best that you should stay it
Not nibble on your ego's dirty bait
Misused, our voice is burdening the world
When aligned, it's love that we've unfurled


## Passing or Failing

The wise don't need the things the unwise crave
The more we would desire the less we know
All inordinate fancy just enslaves
No recipe for the one that wants to grow
In life, desire's the test of everyone
Reactions affect the future of our soul
Each has a different test that they need won
We each have varied ways to realize goals
By God's grace, our tests are clear at first
With occasion to show our selves approved
To ignore or fail means desire's sea walls burst
But passing means inordinate desire's removed
It's really our call how hard we make our life
Passing or failing becomes our karmic* knife

## Pay Attention

We fill our minds with constant commentary
Reliving the past again is just the start
Every variant known with us on top
Thoughts of 'now' an infinitesimal part
Most 'right now' thought has a negative slant
Critiquing other souls that cross our path
Or everything about our situation
Can earn a bit of analytical wrath
Take some time to note how little thought
Can any way be viewed as positive spin
Always contradicting and annulling
Not the course of one who wants to win
Pay attention, hold your tongue and weigh
Within your heart the effect of what you say


## Pay Heed

Consciousness becomes just what we eat
The science of Yin* and Yang, manifest
Indulgent eating's based in self-conceit
Discipline shows the soul more self-possessed
Elements in all our food transfer to us
The nutritional core of every single cell
Its quality shows us drained or more robust
Healing or hurting our outer, mortal shell
For every food contains its own vibration
Which continues once it's been ingested
Forming vibrant layers or stagnation
Our energy's amply flowing, or congested
With your mouth pay heed to what's put in
It points to future health or one's chagrin

## Persevere

Failing nine times
Success on the tenth
Perseverance a noble trait
If after nine times
You called it a day
Your victory you'd abdicate

## Point of Power

Every moment's full of God-potential
As is all that we may gaze upon
In our day and age this is essential
Before our civilization's too far gone
We each can individually set the tone
A wholeness filling our in- and outer space
What's then revealed is what we've always known
Limitation is what we should replace
Sense the flow that always starts within
Colored by our present frame of mind
Our disposition extends beyond our skin
Positive change occurs when all's aligned
Be silent as concerns this gift revealed
The present's the point of power now unsealed

## Poised at Our Core

There's a place 'tween centered and askew
Between our feeling blocked or in the flow
Our state of faith does help us passing through
Dry spells when we don't seem quite aglow
Pulsation is a signature of life
But expectation impedes this constant flow
The result is inner tension and more strife
Denying the soul its innate need to grow
Balance is the essence of this way
The mortar of a solid, pure foundation
These spirals of pulsation will not stray
Into paths of disarray's creation
Change will not be something we abhor
When power, wisdom and love's poised at our core

## Prepare to Become Aware

So busy are we with our life each day
Too busy for what God's ordained for us
Depleted by our energies gone astray
A pause could help in strengthening our trust
If our day's so full, we never realize
We're too busy to listen or to care
Too intent to stop and recognize
We've just passed by an angel unaware
Too involved to do the things we should
For life is moving fast, the pace is great
We always think we would then if we could
But if we pause it's sure to make us late
When our daily schedule means so much
With the voice of God we're out of touch

In part, the work of those who wish us ill
Is confusing what's important in our life
They up the pace on lifestyle's trendy mill
The calm within pushed out by bale* and strife
We still keep saying, there'll come a time some day
A day, in fact, which never does arrive
Then we'll do what till then we've delayed
When there's time for more than just survive
As long as we continue in this way
Listening to the world's distorted voice
Our higher self will seem so far away
Our soul is surely making the wrong choice
As we each surrender to God's plan
We become His 'tool' to help all man

Don't obviate the good that we do now
Or think there's just no time for any more
As we surrender, God will show us how
His full potential to us He'll outpour
Our narrow vision sets us in our ways
The prison bars our mind does put us in
We notice not just how our energy strays
Instead of moving on we're in a spin
Our time and space which now seems to enchant
Are illusions when they're viewed above
By drawing upon His light we'll soon recant
Doing what before was just unheard of
As His love infuses what we do
Our full potential's spilling forth anew

If we're sincere in all that we desire
No other motive then can e'er hold sway
All of heaven with us will conspire
Opportunities presented every day
For all it really takes to e'er accomplish
What we might have thought beyond our rank
Is faith in God, no human 'make-a-wish'
With a heart that's humble, filled with thanks
At this time decide who you will serve
This will not work, if you're on the fence
For heaven gives us all that we deserve
It's much more than a mere coincidence
God knows when we're giving it our all
Then He gives to us His true windfall

We can push back all that would confine
Limits are what we alone accept
There's no place, on this heavenly vine
For those who fear, all life seems windswept
As we through our doubt deplete God's light
Turning decisions made this way and that
We'll confine His mantle*, our birthright
Veiled potential hid beneath our hat
As our thought and actions emanate
From the silent chamber that's within
We sense just what our soul would thus create
As the veil that clouds begins to thin
In our heart we'll know that it is true
As our life takes on this heavenly hue

For in truth, there's really no great difference
All is part and parcel of the One
Our human mind would try to state a preference
Dividing up what heaven's wholly spun
If all we did was spotless in its motive
Then God, through His grace, would reveal
Perfection would impel us how to live
Imbuing every moment with His zeal
If we as Peter walking on the water
For a moment let in fear and doubt
His sinking 'neath the waves would then occur
With us as our efforts would burn out
Only through a true and full surrender
Does Spirit's middle way reveal its splendor

Meditate upon this point of contact
This holy place where God's perfection reigns
Much more valid than our worldly abstract
This purest realm of infinite domains
The clarity of this reverential vision
Takes some time to fully learn to use
Returns us to that place as the Christ son
His flame of wisdom helps us rightly choose
To bless and consecrate all we would do
Instills God's love right through our radiant Chi*
The path is walked each day as we imbue
A mantle of perfection all may see
We're God's representative here below
Expanding as a seven-hued* rainbow

Transformed by the willingness to give
This fire glows with omnipresent heat
This ray within, of light, is very active
Our sacrifice helps make us more complete
This fervent inner fire's what propels us
To levels whole, and to victories won
What's fearful it will surely turn to trust
As evil cowers 'fore this mighty Sun
All giving creates motion in the heart
His eternal fire's passing through
Raising us to levels quite apart
As vibration's raise, we become renewed
When giving of our heart, affirm what's true
This mantle is endowed with cosmic view

Expand, expand this flame of joy within
Perfection fills the moments of our day
New wine is poured to fill our auric* 'skin'
With fragrance as a heavenly bouquet
Blessing all we see and all we touch
A Buddhic mien of peace expands each day
God's sphere of light will purify as such
As we're climbing higher straightaway
Excelsior and victory, plain to see
Thy immortal command, "All is One"
Arrayed in light as God's made us to be
He saw what He had made and said "Well done"
Hallelujah as we beam with light
A glory that's stepped down from heaven's height

## Pride

For those who think they know it all
Life's a droughty brook
No wisdom gained
No wherewithal
Their pride is their textbook

## Pride's Unbearable Fire

Be not aloof with other parts of life
Spiritual pride is such a terrible weight
Just how on earth, can you know it all?
And what got you to nibble on that bait?
We walk the restless path of our caprice
Holding tattered rags of human vanity
Pursued at the expense of inner peace
And often, of our soul's instinctive sanity
Lack of humility is such a dangerous match
Kindling spiritual pride's unbearable fire
If the soul decides to then attach
It's then put on a sordid, vile attire
There's nothing that needs proving to the world
But a humble mien that's thus unfurled


## Proving Ground

The preservation of truth occurs through action
Not by intellect alone
In philosophic abstraction
When made concrete, we thus become
The fullness of its part and sum
A budding of the seed that we have sown

Hypocrisy is the result of only thinking
Then the truth's untested
Just some vain hoodwinking
The tangible is the proving ground
Making theory whole and sound
Food's no benefit to us undigested

## Resolve It

When our stomach's topped off full of food
There's a wall in front of inner senses
An alteration as well, of one's mood
Becoming one of nature's worst offenses
Not found in habits of our animal friends
Is this pattern of our overeating
For gluttony is the path that does offend
Our bodies get a burden and a beating
Food is not for soothing our emotions
Relieving those frustrations set upon us
Liable are we now for this commotion
Ignoring God, our bridge of inner trust
Deal with that conundrum without chewing
Resolve it, food is all that should be stewing


## Rut or Groove

If each of us would take the time
And weigh within our heart
Where in life's the line for keeping
The rut and groove apart

For by a simple turn of thought
Our life turns to and fro
There's times when we all need to plant
New seeds to help us grow

The fear of changing what we do
Is the basis for a rut
'In the groove' requires nuance
To shift or turn somewhat

We need the courage to explore
What makes our muses tick
Change bound to a solid core
Creates a life that clicks

With restraint in our desires
And vigilance in our mien
We'll find our life then flowing upward
Radiant and pristine

## Sacred Art of the Ancients

Almost all the people
Almost all the time
Are unaware of breathing
Causing health to decline

The only time there's awareness
Of what's in- or exhaled
Is if congestion's disrupting
And normalcy's assailed

Voluminous conscious breathing
Invigorating to the soul
By filling up our capacity
One is recharged and whole

So much more can go in
And so much more can come out
Most of our breathing is tepid
Not what vitality's about

Not esoteric or difficult
This refining of our breath
The first thing done in life
The last thing 'fore our death

Pay just a little attention
To this somatic* succession
The easiest way to prevention
The simplest way to refreshen

Invigorating when deep and fast
Calming when deep and slow
Prana's* a form of nourishment
To heal and help us grow

The more we're consciously aware
Of how to effectively breathe
The more we will then benefit
From what this practice bequeaths

By awakening to this gift
Of the art of how to respire
Just focusing our attention
Is all it really requires

The benefits are enormous
In the physical and emotional
Our nature's then more focused
Charged, or calm and devotional

This sacred art of the ancients
Needs reviving today
Restoring divinity's wholeness
Pranayama's* devotee


**Sacred Honor**

May your life be found a path of honor
Sacrificing to its flame held high
In your heart no virtue should be fonder
To no other mantle thus apply
For each one's sense of duty raises all
By truth's beacon that our Lord's defined
Neglecting such a calling should appall
The fulfillment of a future so sublime
Standing on one's precepts held so dear
Dear within the sanctum of one's heart
Life's holy purpose now made clear
From His blessed will, do not depart
Define the course and tenor of your way
As your sacred honor's on display

## See Clearly

Preconceived notions cloud the mind
Obscure the nature of our true reality
Obsessions, good or bad, always blind
Entangled in reaction and duality
These self-imposed blinders color truth
Cutting one off from Spirit's true perspective
Stress and pain become the living proof
Our human sense is never that effective
To contemplate and sit in meditation
Transcends all confusion here below
This heightened point of view's our liberation
From those snarls that always block our flow
Being wide and open to God's word
Sharpens sight which at one time was blurred


## Serving from the Heart

In kindness shown to others, first things first
It's never for applause or some reward
Be the offered cup when others thirst
Our good that's done is like a sacred sword
All blessings are in giving, not receiving
Openings abound for all who are awake
Expecting recompense is so deceiving
Is our offering simply for our sake?
The greatest gift is giving of one's self
Filling needs in life as they appear
The talents we possess are heaven's wealth
To help create a loving atmosphere
Serving from the heart can be devout
What, in truth, all service is about

## Share the Gift

When we see a talent we desire
We're smaller than that skill that's in our view
Mastery of that talent will then show
We're greater than the gift that we accrue
To only hold this capacity we've secured
Slowly shall it dim our inner power
Stowing talents means we've thus insured
Our soul is what it slowly will devour
By absorbing what we now have thus acquired
And sharing what's been placed upon our heart
We rise above it, reaping heaven's fire
To the higher step He would impart
By serving life with all we do receive
To His heart our soul shall ever cleave*


## Sideways to Reality

There's times we all get sideways to reality
When our life won't seem to gel or flow
We've lost the crest and wave of God's totality
Standing still though all we do is row
We've begun a phase of slip and slide
The clarity of His presence is diffused
Turbulence has jolted our smooth ride
Chances for getting it right have been misused
Throughout our day there's not a situation
That doesn't offer options left and right
By settling in our pool of lamentation
Our ego's in control of heaven's light
Never let a moment pass us by
Asleep to a circumstance's why

# Silence

Though words will have their time when deftly* placed
Our silence should be what we most revere
There's times when what's been said should be erased
Better if those words would disappear

The calm that's then created by our silence
A strength for all to build upon and grow
Gossip is a mud that we dispense
And silence is God's manner here below

Those who always chatter waste potential
Through their ignorance, all that light is lost
Silence begets a harmony most essential
Tapping into vistas yet uncrossed

Many spoken words will limit power
Let points be made with meager words or less
Silence helps attunement to then flower
Touching hearts with heaven's sweet caress

As the space that silence has grows fatter
Attention must be centered on our God
Or those voids are filled with carnal chatter
Over silken light rays it does trod

Ask the pearl shell what creates its content
"What pray tell does make you so disposed?"
The response received is truly heaven sent
"It's silence, you see, for years my lips were closed"

## Silence is the Canvas

Start with meditation on pure silence
Imbibe this hallowed essence that's within
Stop to hear what's in your aural space
Without a thought, gently take it in
Silence resonates in our sentient field
The womb of all our outward-based creation
Reawaken what till now's been sealed
And read the book of cosmic ideation
By then intoning sacred tone and verse
With visualization through the inner eye
A lifetime of our density's then reversed
As disparate parts of self are unified
Let silence be the plane on which we paint
The question's will our vision bless or taint?

## Simplify

Simplify all eating to renew
Most just overdo it every day
A lot of common thought is so untrue
More than not it's leading one astray
Less is always better than some more
Especially with variety and with volume
Combine this with repetitive chews galore
Getting more from less than you'd assume
Indulging in the edibles we desire
Is a habit poisoning our whole system
To diet's timeless truths we must aspire
And find a more pure and vital stratagem
To violate nature's laws is not real smart
In time, one's health and peace will come apart

## So August

Eating less
And chewing more
The method for feeling robust
One must confess
It's not folklore
But the way to start feeling august*


## Solve That Problem

Does eating solve that problem or just hide it?
You'd never know, the way some stuff it in
"It doesn't work", the answer of those who've tried it
Seek a different mode for peace within
Doubt removes clear seeing from our souls
Moil* and fear's the fruit of hesitation
Food can't pull one out of self-made holes
It has no part in solving life's equation
To humbly be at peace with all right now
Giving sans reserve with all our might
Simple physical effort creates know-how
As answers to our crises come forthright
Resolve is born of confidence, faith and action
Food can't be the rope for our extraction


## Sow Peace

Say what you need to say
But always speak with kindness
So much of what is spoken
Comes from spiritual blindness

A word's a knife or balm
Depending upon our heart
What's said can love and affirm
Or with cunning, tear apart

Realize how consequential
Is the nature of our voice
At all times and places
Let harmony be the choice

Bite that acerbic tongue
There's a better way to phrase it
Promoting peaceful strains
The finesse of how we raise it

Tolerance of a view
Different than our own
Civility to ensue
Starting with our tone

We'll never really grow
If all we want to hear
Are the thoughts that we believe
Naught outside our sphere

Most have an innate view
Formed in that one's mind
To find a common ground
We must not speak purblind

For those who demand to hear
What they perceive is right
Sets them up as unjust
Appearing vain and trite

To be a flame of love
Reject all vain conceit
Let the tongue and heart be joined
Sow peace with all you meet

## Spiral of Civility

Politeness is inner kindness
That's outwardly expressed
Expanding the love within
As all of life is blessed

The one of humble mien
Sees every soul's true self
That one's God-potential
That one's inner wealth

For no one's any better
And no one's any worse
Sincere consideration
The joy that we disperse

By seeing each one's potential
Not deeming them too low
Our respectful demeanor
Sets that one aglow

Then that one reciprocates
Wherever they may go
This spiral of civility
Has an afterglow

We each can make a difference
With everyone we meet
We'll see that love and kindness
Helps make the world complete

## Stay Centered in His Love

We see just where we are
There's where we want to be
The gulf that we must cross
Is fraught with mystery

Those rocky crags that form
The mountain that we see
Can dash the soul to pieces
Or raise to victory

Know every single instance
Every moment of the day
Is put there for a reason
In the hope that it conveys

That life is like a staircase
Our experiences are the stairs
We decide the direction
Petitioning God with prayers

Sometimes all seems clear
At times a cloud of mystery
Without His light to guide us
Our direction's hard to see

By envisioning our goal
Staying centered in the heart
We'll know events outplayed
Are playing an essential part

To guide or encourage
To dissuade or instruct
By maintaining attunement
They'll never more obstruct

For if our desire's pure
We're aligned with God's law
Then how things outplay
Seems right without a flaw

But the fly in the ointment
Is human thought and feeling
Disturbing the pristine waters
Lowering God's boundless ceiling

If we so determine
To stay centered in His Love
Then all that we experience
Will emanate from above


## Take a Closer Look

To sense that we are sated once we've eaten
Means that we should take a closer look
Our body shouldn't feel it's stuffed or beaten
But answers won't be found in any book
We each will need to spend some quality time
In the inner workshop of our person
The amount and type of foods that keep us prime
And just which kinds of viands* seem to worsen
Since each and every one is so unique
No common blanket theory covers all
It always takes some time to reach one's peak
With discipline, insight and wherewithal
With some Macro* theory under your belt
You'll soon be feeling the best you've ever felt


## Take Charge

We're thinking we have freedom, but we don't
Our psychology's become the bulwark of our cell
We need to face reality, but we wont
By observing and correcting, one can tell

But the log within our eye can use more time
Not our brother's mite* that does absorb us
We all have lots of work to be sublime
With others' lives we needn't make a fuss

For what some bear is world sin, not their own
Through their burdens others may then grow
Hardships borne that someone may atone
Our condemnation packs a heavy blow

No one is a victim without flaws
Their past has now returned, the payments due
No one here can ever know the cause
Passing judgment's not a God-virtue

Compassion for all others is God's way
Walk that mile, in another's shoes
We all enter life with debts to pay
Decisions, good and bad, are what accrue

Change is part of everyone's potential
We're each the only one who can refine it
No one else can tell us what's essential
Take charge, as God's love helps you define it

## Temptation

Each day we're served a new plate of desire
Be it revenge, power, sex or food
The path to take for any who aspire
Is of a humble, loving attitude
Heaven takes a notice when we stand
For principles in our heart we know are true
God will disengage us strand by strand
Erasing the fractured picture that we drew
All He ever asks in compensation
For any tempted by desire's wrath
Is our ever-loving supplication
And staying upon His pure and narrow path
Think of God when bothered by temptation
The answer for our victory and purgation*

## Ten Noble Actions

*One*
Seek after God
There's no other striving
He's life's only goal
All else is depriving

*Two*
Search after wisdom
It illumines the way
The guide, without whom
All progress we delay

*Three*
The 'now' is our teacher
For it matters not
Whom or whatever
Life has thus begot

*Four*
Obedience to the teacher
Submit to the wise
Life's wisdom transfer
To help one thus cognize

*Five*
Renounce all trifling
Curb all trite pursuits
If they don't bring wholeness
All verity it then dilutes

*Six*
Be pious and continent
In all words and deeds
Comply with His law
Life's most sacred creeds

*Seven*
By submitting to the path
We gain serenity
Surrendering's divine
When by God's decree

*Eight*
Reticence* is good
Taciturn's way
By speaking very little
Our inner voice conveys

*Nine*
Vigilance is needed
Thus sleep very little
If the truth be told
Enlightenment's in the middle

*Ten*
Self-restraint in diet
Espouse the temperate way
By eating very little
There's no ebb or sway

These are the hallmarks
Which enlighten our life's path
Ten holy principles
For binding moil's* wrath

To diligently obey them
Will help us reach our goal
Truth is then made manifest
Joy and peace to extol

But if we're found deficient
In as little as one
We can rest assured
Our victory won't be won

## Tests of Truth

O baneful human pride
So hollow with its lies
Puffing the soul way up
All truth it crucifies

Convinced of its importance
A special place within
Humility's not a factor
On its way to ruin

Take these tests of truth
To find the self approved
Nothing is a given
What's false we must reprove

If God gets adoration
Morning, noon and night
Nothing else holds interest
The world moves on in spite

Give God first the glory
Then all is added on
No other gods before Him
To cast His light upon

There's no time we're off
When perfecting our soul
A desire to get away
Means God's just not the goal

Pulsing in and out
Sometimes hot or cold
Constancy's what's needed
As all the saints of old

Moderation in all things
To walk the middle way
If we're overdoing it
It's done to God's dismay

Prayer and invocation
Affirmation and decree
If our heart's not in it
Its rote and fantasy

There's no one else but God
Knowing what we do
The ignoring of this law
Our good just won't accrue

Abrasive times in life
Are for polishing the soul
If blaming any others
There's debit in our bankroll

For there's nothing and no one
That we can ever blame
That causes our agitation
It's the same old carnal game

These are guideposts on the path
But there's danger that it poses
'Cause pride will make us think
Everything smells like roses

Only true contrition
With a humble heart in tow
Can overcome the obstacles
Our ego's bound to throw

The more these are a part
Of our consciousness and world
The more our soul moves toward
The ascension's flame unfurled

## This Business of Living

This business of living is a great adventure
Don't be bored as humdrum tags along
We needn't ever feel that we're indentured
We should make all life a graceful song
But educated vision's what it takes
Shedding all distortion that's not real
When we take the foot off our life's breaks
We then become imbued with righteous zeal
We tend to love the illusions of the mind
Contortions of our lean imagination
These ephemeral shadows are what bind
Leading slowly to our soul's stagnation
Impossible is no word that God would know
To strike it from our soul will help us grow


## Through the Heart

With our brain there's many faults to see
Through the heart a purer vision held
We control our joy or misery
All contrary thoughts should be dispelled
Intellect and eye discern distinction
The ear and heart will tend to unify
Every soul's a unique variation
Though really not enough to qualify
Unity is found below the surface
More agrees than tends to meet the eye
Apply the heart to atrophy much less
Completeness is what pure love magnifies
If we base our vision through the heart
We'll tend to see the whole and not the part

## To Grow in Every Situation

Do something you don't want to do each day
For that is where our soul is tested most
This discipline we have gleaned will e'er repay
A confidence-builder and a clear guidepost
Procrastination's source is sloth or fear
Things to overcome and not avoid
Nothing's as overwhelming as appears
If we're attuned then all can be enjoyed
The strength to grow in any situation
Is the higher mind's dowry* to the soul
No circumstance should lead to a negation
For never could that be an ordained goal
Sense the woof* and flow of each event
Then each affair will grace and not torment


## Transcendence

Everyone at times does need a change
Complacency is not the way to grow
The secret is in how we each arrange
Elements of each day's perfect flow
The source of initiation's found within
Conscious efforts tend to go astray
Not a place for 'coulda', 'shoulda' been
All doubt and fear is guaranteed dismay
The magic of the present's where to start
That's the point of power on life's path
Effulgent inspiration from the heart
A sense of 'new', the blessed aftermath
Transcendence makes our life unique and whole
That we may surely strive to reach our goal

## True Character

One's true character
Comes out in the wash
In times of adversity
Will harmony get squashed?

When times are good
It's easy to say
"I'm in control"
Coming off blasé

But when all hits the fan
Then what do we do?
As our boiling point's reached
All harmony eschew

Problems are tests
We hope we will pass
But if not set in harmony
They start to amass

The time to judge character
Is up against trouble
Coming up roses
Or bursting our bubble

When all can then pass
Without a rise
We're allowing harmony
To crystallize

Then we can say
Our character's true
Harmony's become
Our blessed virtue

## Truly Awakened

Most adults still carry 'parts' of children
With added bills and much more obligation
Re-living interactions once again
The more they hurt the deeper their pulsation
Formative years are critical to each one's growth
Those fears, loves and joys still carry on
The buried keys to present fears and wroth*
Unless confronted, they're never really gone
A false security's the reason they remain
For all our guardians cast a shadow long
Re-enacting roles when under strain
Repeating unawares the same old song
To cling to puerile* phobias stunts the soul
Sleepwalking through our life, the sorry toll

## Tumbleweed or Stone

Some are fine just blowing in the wind
While ironclad gives others their security
In truth we must perceive the need for balance
Poised 'tween Yin* and Yang shows soul maturity
Returning to fixed goals by holy wisdom
In our lives so prudent, wise and apt
But free to row the currents of life's stream
Shows that one is able to adapt
The conducting of our soul is most essential
And open to God, guiding where He would
Commitment to then consecrate our purpose
Holding firm or moving when we should
Since there's no soul that's tumbleweed or stone
The middle way will show that we have grown

## Turn Within

Each circumstance will breed its own solution
No test is given that we cannot pass
Doubt and fear are forms of foul pollution
Which keep us in a bewildering morass
This disconnect, comes from our neglect
It's our density blocking waves of light
Thinking we're forgotten's incorrect
To help us out would be God's great delight
But when our consciousness is far away
We loose the pulse and rhyme of our existence
The inner answers now can't be conveyed
Succumbing to the outer world's resistance
Turn within, not out, to problem solve
And watch this union strengthen and evolve

## Violet Flame

There is a science of divine healing
Restoring wholeness to a burdened soul
To those with open hearts it is revealing
It helps us each to reach our final goal
This holy science is of transmutation
Restoring pristine wholeness both in and out
It never works with doubt or trepidation
But with faith creates our turnabout
Visualize your problem bathed in violet
The highest vibration in our color hue
This purplish pink has miracles to beget
With constant use its blessings will accrue
Repeat, "I AM* a being of violet fire"
With, "I AM the purity God desires"

## Vision Clear

Many seek to be what they are not
Illusions and delusions so abound
And most, also know not what they've got
The light of God on which their being's wound
Problems rise when in and out don't match
All stunted growth curves in upon itself
The soul perplexed will slowly then detach
From what's real to touch what's vague and stealth
To over- or under-appraise one's opinion
Of what that one would feel that it deserves
Are they a king or just a lowly minion
The refined course or just a plain hors d'oeuvre
The humble soul arrayed with God-reality
Has vision clear not living in duality


## The Voice of God, the Song of Life

Know the hallowed voice of God
Through the rustling of the leaf
In the rolling clap of thunder
And waves kissing the massif

Language is our vain attempt
To digest the voice of God
Sacred music brings us closer
To piercing life's façade

We're each a perfect note of music
Within our terrestrial realm
Our keynote ever sounds our essence
Though inaudible, it does whelm

We in Him, Him in us
Light's ineffable domain
As we sing our song of life
Let it be a celestial strain

161

The voice of God, the song of life
Intoned throughout each day
Resonate with harmony's light
As burdens fall away


## Walk the Fine Line

We need to walk the fine line
'Tween hunger and being sated
Our energy is more refined
And this is all related

By giving our body just
The minimal amount it needs
Strengthens a sacred trust
Purity's what it breeds

The lighter our daily fare
The smoother our systems run
Helps us then prepare
To know our I AM* 'sun'

The less we're filled with food
The more we resonate
A positive attitude
Pure thoughts to contemplate

Though our food's essential
It needs be pure and whole
To realize full potential
Amounts should be controlled

If we learn to breathe
As the saints have done
What it will bequeath
Are meals not overdone

We imbibe nothing more
In our physical domain
That affects the core
Of the health that we retain

But breathing is an art
Passed down through many ages
Makes us more a part
Of the attunement of the sages

Breathing lessens hunger
Revivifies or stills
Gets one feeling younger
The answer to our ills

Breathing and chewing more
Will get one eating less
And open up the door
To chill and decompress

When aware of in- and exhaling
We're learning what's essential
Then we'll soon be scaling
The heights of our potential


## Walk This Way

Some clear night, with stars arrayed
Go out for a leisurely stroll
The good this walk does thus convey
To you I now extol

Look not around, look not beneath
But silently step the way
The solemn stillness, will bequeath
Good thoughts as when we pray

This tranquil, eventide serenity
Sooths and calms the soul
Healing one's strife and enmity*
A view of life that's whole

The beauty of this steady motion
With lungs so full of air
Recedes to quiet, all commotion
Relief from life's harsh glare

A winding down to set the tone
For a night of blissful sleep
Before it's through one's burdens have flown
Our rest's now calm and deep

A simple way to find new peaks
And foster a sound attitude
Gives command to the one that seeks
And a heart of gratitude

## What is Most Important

There comes a time in each and every life
When we wonder, why'd that happen to me?
What did I do to claim this pain and strife
And finally, how may I then best foresee?
Our life first gives us signs so very small
Subtle clues that we have gone astray
Over time the signs grow mean and tall
Until our soul wakes up and we obey
No answer found in money or repute
Nor in the sanction of our kin and friends
For truth is something we simply can't refute
To follow it puts our burdens on the mend
What is then of most import to know
Is what in truth our spirit needs to grow

## What You See

Observe the features of our fellow man
Some are cast in beauty, strength and poise
This reflects a disciplined life-long plan
Features thus are formed with equipoise*
Others have their features strained and broken
Carrying abuses of their thought and feeling
A burdened past, and now their life has spoken
Their punished image needs be self-revealing
Know wholeness is our spirit's ordered form
Godly expression's symmetry manifest
Creating patterns of beauty is the norm
Know balance is our spirit's final test
Like the solar cycles and each season
Life's defined by God's perfected reason

## When We Eat Too Much

When we eat too much
It becomes a crutch
And we waste our energy away
By eating less
We'll have to confess
Daylong, it surely does pay

## Who and What We Are

We deserve no more than what we have
Thinking counter is but human folly
A crystallized driving bent both good and bad
The source of all our joy and melancholy
The 'yes, but' syndrome causes all our pain
Non-acceptance bears our painful blight
Acceding to our abetment is a start
Then disparate thoughts and feelings can unite
Human expectation sets a course
With self-seeking, casts an ugly pall
A constant disconnect is now in place
A spiral that will lead to our downfall
We've created who and what we are
Not any other person near or far

## Words

The words that we would speak are as a seed
Sprouting in the womb of that one's heart
Attunement says if we shoot straight or cede
At times we seem not consciously a part
Words express the quality of our soul
Our tone of voice reflects our inner landscape
If clarity in thoughts and feelings is the goal
Harmony's what our voice must always shape
Let the words we speak be very few
As our mind and heart expand with love
By speaking less whatever's said rings true
A stronger union with our God above
Words convey the essence of our core
Not something to take lightly or ignore

## Wrinkled or Smooth

To smooth out every wrinkle from our day
Seems a task beyond our scope and range
Awareness is the iron to hold sway
'Thinking' with our heart affects the change
Perspective sets what seems so creased or smooth
A joyous, tranquil mind becomes our iron
We control what agitates or soothes
Setting the parameters of our peace environ
Wrinkles are the things that stir our embers
Along with where we think we ought to be
Life's creases start to fade if one remembers
This view means our attunement is off-key
If body, heart and soul are sitting right
Peace of mind's maintained, come what might

## Your Stock-In-Trade

Find three points of strength and thus attainment
Three points where you excel
With honor's glorious raiment
Esteem with true nobility
And day-to-day constancy
Trust that you may effectively compel

Find three points of woe and limitation
Three points where you fall short
Causing consternation
Character flaws to eliminate
Not fluff off and procrastinate
And slowly all your peace of mind contort

Be ever mindful of these signals six
Constant progress made
End carnal lies and tricks
Self-transcending for all time
As life becomes much more sublime
Finding truth's become your stock-in-trade

## Youthfully Grow Old

To learn to naturally play the hand we're dealt
Macrobiotics* and yoga sure make sense
Clear and vibrant, the best we've ever felt
Done at disease and lethargy's expense
These miracle ways have an ancient wellspring
Universal concepts from the East
A science tying in most everything
As self-sustained burdens are released
Each individual's regimen is unique
We're all different from our fellow man
Though optimum health is what we all do seek
Our age, sex and lifestyle tweak the plan
It's time to learn to youthfully grow old
As the venerable teachers have foretold

# 3
# Truth & Freedom

## A Drop of Ink

A drop of ink
Can make millions think
But what are they thinking about?
The dissemination
Of disinformation
Or truth and the freedom it sprouts?

## A God for Everyone

To all in life who try to live
God's truth upon life's way
Know it's not which path you choose
Or how you pray each day

Our common source is held within
Known deep within each heart
The attributes pure hearts bestow
Should unite, not pull apart

The eyes, the windows of the soul
Reveal those on truth's way
It does not matter which altar used
Or the words they say

Each one of us begins our life
Embodied East or West
The home instills the foundation for
Which path for each is best

But religions of the modern day
Have thwarted divine love
For power, pride, prestige and wealth
Lost favor from above

This climb upon God's mountain path
Is for each soul to grow
Not throwing stones and arguments
Of who does really know

For all who with a humble heart
Show love to everyone
Will know, despite dogmatic reign
God's voice that says "Well done!"

True seekers on the path of love
Go within to find our God
And all without shall harmonize
A love-inspired jihad*

To those who hate, defame and kill
That never is God's way
No glory's found at that road's end
All truth they do betray

His love unites our disparate ways
A ray of cosmic sun
Restoring peace on our earth home
A God for everyone


**A Moral Resurrection**

Force will not give rise to moral validity
Might will never, ever, equal right
When will we say enough to our leaders' stupidity?
Bureaucracy's become this nation's blight
The ultimate right to fend the public good
Occurs when we the citizens take a stand
Too much idle talk of should and would
Prattle never made a nation grand
Legal power's a part of common trust
No rights are gained by legalistic coups
Tort reform has now become a must
With our inner sanction of innate truths
We the people shape this land's direction
Let it start with a moral resurrection!

# The Age of Truth

Beloved Father, with us through each age
Within worldwide cultures thus adored
Loved by the pure and not, saint and sage
Call Him Brahma, Allah, Jehovah, Lord

Thou center of all, least understood
By our human consciousness so confined
To sense that God is with us is all good
When life does bend us toward the dense and blind

Bless all those walking in a darkened state
With attunement to know their good from ill
Bind the lies of pre-ordained fate
And fathom all the blessings of free will

Awaken the conscience to all that needs be done
And by Thy inner prompts, what not to do
What's needed, rather than a hell to shun
Is knowing heaven's in us to pursue

Quicken us all, to Thy way perceived
That our ignorance may not cast away
Holding fast to what we have received
The truest peace found in Thy will obeyed

May we hold not to this earthly span
For Thy graciousness does so abound
Or bind Thee only to the sentient man
For all's created by Thy natal sound

Stay our weak, unknowing, fearful hands
As each faith will have its stone to throw
That they cast their ignorance 'round the land
Judging those that they perceive as foe

Illuminate what's right, Thy grace impart
By Thy will, that each soul may not stray
If wrong, may you then, teach their heart
Becoming illumined to Thy better way

May a humble heart cease foolish pride
Or a trite and petty discontent
When found aloof, Thy wisdom is denied
As Thy sacred energies fly misspent

Teach us to always sense another's woe
Ignoring all the faults we think are there
Know mercy then, that we to others show
Will be our hallowed works accrued fore'er

Though this world has evil, not wholly so
As each is quickened by Thy sacred breath
Guide all upon this path of earthly woe
Our victory rendered over sin and death

We pray that peace may ever be our lot
Brotherhood mastered through Thy blessed Son
As evil's heinous plans, come to naught
Not mastered by our will but Thine be done

Let this world become a hallowed space
Manifest throughout the lands, seas and skies
Become a beautiful chorus, one faith, one race
As the Age of Truth does surely rise

## All Our Help's Within

Attainment's path's not found in any book
A book on sleep will never give one rest
But thinking so will make us bait to hook
We're in the next improvement guru's nest
Lives are bound in varied levels of ignorance
Depends on what's been drawn from inner truth
Our state is gauged by our enlightened beneficence
Thus serving life becomes our living proof
Our absorption in books on self-improvement
Becomes every procrastinator's dream
The feedback of real life is always absent
This 'help', at times a money-making scheme
If the truth were known, our help's within
Those experts then would take it on the chin

## Angel Bands

From God on high there comes a band
Glorious angels to guide our hand
Rays of light from heavenly hold
Crowning glory to the stout and bold

Counts of infinity around Him still
To sing His praise and do His will
Ever ready when called to go
Protect and inspire us here below

The Lord's command to them each day
Is guide each soul upon life's way
Escort all souls in sleep each night
To and from the schools of light

All angels don't do good and right
Some have fallen from heaven's height
Those who inspire us most each day
Define which motives in us hold sway

A pure heart keeps God's angels near
Strength and support through doubt and fear
And at life's end they guide us home
To reunite in the heavenly Om*

## Awakening

Too many float through all their daily events
Dream-walkers on this path that we call life
When consciousness quickens, that's what then prevents
Their banging against the walls of bane and strife
For a constellation of change does then occur
The mind, senses, heart and soul awaken
This arousing of the heart will soon bestir
How their life has slowly been misshapen
It's hard to imagine there's a heightened state
When most are taken by their waking dream
All the 'ifs' and 'buts' of dull debate
Will not deny the soul this inner gleam
To awaken unifies self, world and God
Stripping away the carnal dream façade

## Become Freedom's Patriots

When will we the people act
Sense the state of freedom's power
Rally to the cause of truth
No longer then just shrink and cower

Not enmeshed in mortal think
With thoughts thus shaped by any other
But being concerned, of God's desire
A harmony found with one another

Playing out our singular role
Spreading freedom upon this earth
We are each an integral part
Of this planet's grand rebirth

Every life's a path of testing
Becoming steadfast in God's eyes
Our life's calling is always gauged
By the truth that one applies

We're given more obligation
When God sees the gains we've made
There comes a purging, purifying
Not one debt is left unpaid

By sincerest efforts made
Of the highest good we know
To whom all we meet, heart to heart
Give support to help them grow

With spirits filled with expectation
With hearts thus filled with inner joy
If not now, then maybe never
Let freedom's legions now deploy

Freedom is our nation's fount
Of all we know and feel is true
And now's the time we must become
Freedom's patriots through and through

**Become the Living Proof**

Heaven's walk is more than to an altar
More than confession's needed to be saved
The test is when we hesitate and falter
How sound, is the road that we have paved?
Alas, in truth, life is not so plain
To idolize another helps us not
Superficial worship is our bane
Most have not a clue of what they've got
Distortion and diluting's what's been done
Ignorance and motives sadly quite impure
Orthodoxy commands it's all or none
The blind leading the blind make things obscure
It's time to reawaken inner truth
Let our lives become the living proof

## Becoming Ennobled

To sense the flame of honor in one's duty
When pulled asunder by this coarsened world
The blessing of our service when well done
Victory's found within the heart unfurled
For one's responsibility shall be tested
A probing of the mettle of one's worth
By standing tall and forthright with God's love
We affirm to life the reason for our birth
Our life's defined by victory over challenge
Doing the best according to our range
All overcoming garners greater light
Expansion through the heaven-earth exchange
Our sense of duty manifests from our God
Becoming ennobled on this mortal sod


## Book of Life

After tampering with all man's come upon
How could any with a cogent mind
Think anything stays inviolable for an eon
It puts our blessed world in such a bind
By translations from the original tongue
The truth of sacred texts is slowly lost
We've lost just how the song was being sung
The inner meaning's been so subtly tossed
Whether nefarious or by vain intent
The end results will add up just the same
The straight and narrow road's been slowly bent
Our lack of guard is mostly what's to blame
The book of life is etched upon our soul
Study it then to surely reach life's goal

178

## Break the Spiral

Materialism's heart is broken not by hammers
Its coldness casts a shadow upon all life
Fire is what softens and enamors
Love is fire and its glowing needs be rife
What we seek from others, offer first
Our example is a matrix to be filled
Be a quenching tap to lips that thirst
Plant our seeds in gardens properly tilled
Materialism's a cancer of the soul
It hardens every heart that comes its way
To break the spiral downward, is the goal
Let desires expand the heart, not embay*
An excess of purchase will not soothe our being
Only a balance sought through inner seeing

## The Core of All of Life

Silence is the voice of all creation
Any sonance is of a lesser tone
Nature is its purest intonation
All discord is what humankind have sown

Music's potential is our purest expression
When it's tethered to nature's laws and way
Its character creates the deepest of impressions
To build or destroy is not just trite hearsay

No matter its source, all sound will coalesce
Into form or awareness that's akin
Its energy will expand or decompress
Atoms and electrons in their native spin

Dense and light are more than nebulous terms
But actual qualities any sound begets
The essence of sounds are creation 'germs'
Analogous to a liquid gel that sets

Human-conjured sound as pitch and beat
Adds another component to this gel
The consciousness of that one will cool or heat
Given energies aligned or flung pell-mell

The laws of nature can't be cast aside
Contemporary din and music has its price
As harshness and decay become allied
God's laws are found unyielding and precise

But silence and the sounds of nature's world
Are keynotes to the music of the spheres
The wind through leaves, the ocean waves that furl
A womb of 'music' to the one that hears

Sacred is the business of all sound
Be mindful of the source of all you hear
We're in a sea of vibration all around
It's the core of all of life that we hold dear


## Courage

Every life's a brand new mission
Sense how yours is special too
We need to go within to find it
And then perceive the higher view

Embrace the calling of our God
No one's closer to our heart
Let our soul be slowly quickened
To all the truth He would impart

Grab life's calling by the reins
Neglect it not or turn aside
Reject the broad and easy way
His inner prompts no more elide*

Cast aside all fear and trembling
The confusion of the human mind
The Rock of Ages is forever
There's no need for searching blind

Everyone, both great and small
Began their signal life the same
Drooling oatmeal on their chin
Soiling diapers their claim to fame

But never thinking, it can't be done
And by the courage God placed within
They forged ahead, nay-sayers be gone
Never thinking what could have been

Courage comes in many colors
It's the conquering of our image small
No one's ever had our gifts
Time to become God's cannonball!

## The Cultural Elite

The essence of classical music has now fled
Though its aural body is preserved
Robotic perfection's what we have instead
For an elitist few, it's now reserved
Primitive's how they see the music world
With traditions purer and older than their own
Close minded to the vision that's unfurled
Clueless till they change their pompous tone
Regurgitating the same old tired scores
The spark of pure creation's gone away
Our future's compromised if we ignore
The laws of life all music must obey
In truth, our cultural elite don't know it all
Their thinking so, will lead to our downfall

## Cultural Rebirth

Modern music
Is noise with a beat
Sophomoric and banal
By the cultural elite

Leading us down
The primrose path
The same regurgitation
With its pomp and wrath

These pied pipers of
Broken hearts and doom
Whining and opining
In their next song it resumes

Foisted upon us
By the three-piece suits
With their network of drones
They're all in cahoots

Each generation
They're takin' it down
Nothing is sacred
True or profound

They're sly as a fox
Doing it by steps
No one notices
It softens and preps

Who's their next 'star'
Who will strut and debase
Wherever we go
We'll see that face

There'll come a time
With this inane stuff
When 'anything goes'
Bumps 'enough is enough'

But who out there
Will take a stand?
Show new directions
From the repetitious and bland

For music can intone
To enlighten and heal
With rhythms and melodies
Raising nobler ideals

Even in this age
Of overproduced din
With our 'stars for a day'
And their jaded spin

You'll find if you look
Past the pop milieu
An alternative diet
With a healthier view

A variety of music
From the East and West
Ancient and modern
Sounds of celeste

Take a moment and turn off
That 'star for a day'
There's other kinds of music
Than today's cliché

Look beyond our shores
To the sounds of this earth
It'll broaden your horizons
For a cultural rebirth

## Cultural Resurrection

Music is the progenitor, of a culture's future
Carrying moral decay, or that culture's cure
Many brush it off, as frivolity and fun
And this conceited decadence, is always being outdone

Ignorance begets ignorance, in what's considered 'good'
Its connection with our soul, is barely understood
More than just pop-culture, with endless songs of 'whine'
Our jazz and classical styles, have helped in our decline

Dissonant introversion, has a price to pay
Ever in search of the curious, has led to our decay
Words like "brilliant" and "genius", flung around to smite*
Rebels becoming heroes, is our cultural blight

Confusion and decay, seems the cause celeb
Without them you're not part of, the industry's marketing web
World music's only considered, if it has the 'beat'
Hyphenated categories, continually made obsolete

Why's this music pumped, through our nation's veins?
With all the twisted messages, most of it contains
It's more than making money, as important as that is
Our nation's sinking values, are championed by the 'biz'

Slick, driving beats, with amped up hyper-bass
Words from vain minds, heard most every place
But none of this would be, if it did not sell
Our appetite for this says, our souls just are not well

Programmed to the youngest, that they may conform
Lowering standards for profit, now's become the norm
Until more understand, that sound creates our world
If formed in confused heads, what's then been unfurled?

We need to take the pulse of, where this nation's headed
Find our bearings 'fore, our heritage is shredded
Going along for the ride with, these minstrels of party and gloom
Means our vestiges of good, are ultimately consumed

The spirit of a child, isn't stained by this plague
But it wont take long, when our morals seem so vague
From where society is now, censorship seems the course
The stopping of this hellfire, right at its very source

But censorship's a blow, upon our freedom's core
Depending on the leaders, it always leads to more
If not censorship, what will cure our ills?
How can the pure and good, be what society instills?

Without a reawakening, of a God-realized truth
The souls in our society, will have no living proof
The standard sought within, needs to be the Christ
Human precepts, till now, just have not sufficed

This standard's universal, not given to one man
The call of every soul, to a higher-ordained plan
If we each would just enkindle, this pure Christ-perfection
It could lead this nation, to a cultural resurrection

### Desire the Infinite

Human desire never has an end
Just a bottomless pit
Precious light expend
Endless, mindless variation
Peace of mind's contamination
The problem's never knowing when to quit

Only one desire really counts
That of knowing God
In ever expanding amounts
All other desires are profane
Cast against the heavenly grain
Shadows of a paltry, trite façade

The soul wearies of this constant charge
With no end in sight
And credit balance large
Averse and foul of heaven's creed
The path of truth it does impede
Desire the infinite instead of what's finite

185

## Do Greater Things

Fairy tales can't bear the present load
Of a world, based in laws divine
Pleading nescience* of this cosmic code
Only guarantees our soul's decline
Mortal danger's found in human pride
So utterly sure that they've got it right
How much of what they know is not applied?
Irregardless, they forge ahead in spite
There're no incongruities in God's law
The big picture's there for all to see
Our Higher Self is who to hold in awe
No one past or present on life's screen
How will we ever do those "greater things"
If not prone to truth and what it brings?


## The 'Dust' We Revere

Business, government and religion are the 'dust'
From the road on which our life proceeds
This road of life's a road of sacred trust
The way of glory and of sacred deeds
This residue is not the road itself
But its source is still that very road
Though dust contains a portion of it's wealth
It's a fraction of the mother lode
Confusing derivatives with the path of life
We're mesmerized by the fraction so contained
This confusion leads to all our pain and strife
Why today we're now so stressed and strained
The 'dust' we revere's a portion of our story
An addendum to our true ascension glory

186

## Employ Your Energy to Change

Vigilance is what it takes to make the grade
No pulsing in and out
For truly we're self-made
No such thing as standing still
We're going up or down life's hill
Some go straight ahead, some roundabout

Apathy and indolence are a wave
Engulfing any soul
Sitting in their 'cave'
Enlightened action's what it takes
Removing the foot upon life's brakes
Determine just what part is in control

Energy's wasted covering our behind
Human vanity plain
Fruit of the carnal mind
The ego casts this sorry mold
A whimpering stroke, not grand and bold
Employ your energy to change and not complain

## Fending Freedom

For those who loath the government's fearsome weight
Placed upon the people of this land
Know we're the ones who opened this floodgate
Surrendered freedom slowly strand by strand

When someone will not take it upon their self
Being responsible for their lot in life
Then government has its 'fix' right off the shelf
Dicing freedom with its 'helping' knife

As our founders claimed in ages past
Freedom and security will not mix
With security's 'weight', the die is cast
Is duty still a part of any fix?

A helping hand and safety start within
With abdication there's a widened void
That void is where the government does begin
As programs paid by us are thus employed

Through indifference, most will take no stand
As our freedoms vanish 'fore our eyes
The Trojan horse of government's 'helping hand'
The poor results expose their naïve lies

The corrupting power of 'solutions' so banal
Seeing just the human in solution
'For our good', Big Brother's rationale
It's nothing more than forced redistribution

Equality's just an avoidance of self-will
Something government structures can't create
Determined by what one's character would instill
Caring doesn't mean exonerate

The color of one's skin, race or creed
Can't ever be the guidepost to then say
The self- anointed can 'help' and we'll accede
As our vestige of self-reliance fades away

There's bitterness with results that are not earned
Surmounting circumstances to thus win
Blanket solutions to problems must be spurned
With its dogma, platitudes and spin

As long as we expect our 'chiefs' to do
What in truth's the people's call alone
Our societal divisions continue to accrue
Which convoluted solutions can't atone

If we will not be silenced with largesse
But take the reins of living in our hands
We'll help to stop this 'good-intents' excess
Fending freedom in this blessed land

## Free Will vs. Destiny

If dharma* becomes our life, we are free
But attunement's found in small and common things
With all we do, let thoughts turn to He
By His strength does every impulse spring
When heart directs the labor of the hands
They're sacred wands that God may raise to heal
Our deeds are purified as we expand
Consecrating our efforts with a seal
The Lord has blest each life in solemn fate
Though every soul's accord does cue the start
The free will versus destiny worn debate
Know it starts and ends in every heart
Sincerity's what does make us rise and glow
With motives pure, that our life may flow


## Freedom's Flame

Sacrifice the corruptible lot of man
For the stainless nature of our God
Cleansing our lower bodies is His plan
His violet flame* consumes our base façade
Not a scheme to duck responsibility
Nor blind leading the blind in common faith
But the crowning of His law in chaste humility
'Putting on the new man', what He saith
But how to rise if we neglect salvation?
Is heard by those whose call is freedom's flame
Wherever the soul is found then on life's station
Affirming the I AM* does become the aim
To live life in a state of self-command
Become a flame of freedom strand by strand

## God-Intoned

The beauty of the perfect word sent forth
Sent forth to fondly touch an unknown heart
Illumines as an emblazoned sacred torch
Drawing together all that's come apart
Any word can burden or give hope
The light behind it helps to shape its meaning
Along with each recipient's range and scope
Sets forth the tenor of what that soul is gleaning
The multiplicity of language throughout the world
Has its genesis in the Word made corporal
For dialect is the Mother tongue imperiled
Its diversity's in the soul becoming immoral
The core of every language and each word
Is God-intoned, the nascent sound unheard

## God's a Mountain

The trend today is turning sanct tradition
Into an anthropomorphic* version of the truth
Being part misguidance and omission
Our planet's state, is the graphic proof
Outer differences are culled in master plans
Making the case that each has got it right
This slander and instigation really spans
Through generations, as a vile apartheid
Though sects and faiths now seem fundamental
They're splinters of an etern truth that's whole
Judgmental now, more than transcendental
Really they're all stating the same goal
The truth is God's a mountain we all climb
We each can make it hell or most sublime

# God's Gift

Going through life, with blinders on
Rejecting what's 'yond our nose
When life's opportunities, have up and gone
What then will we propose?

So many people, will only hear
Just what they agree with
They're always the easiest, ones to steer
By any deceptive myth

Like the parachute in, the teaching tale
Only effective unfurled
A closed-up mind, is self-betrayal
When open, a brand new world

Our growth comes, from drawing in
Many divergent views
The more we assimilate, from within
The less confusion ensues

All experience, and interaction
Has divine intent
Shutting down, is soul contraction
Avoiding what's heaven sent

Holistically viewing, all of life
Unifies disparate ways
Serenity found, instead of strife
Is what this path conveys

When we hear, divergent thought
Instead of fighting back
It's another piece, in life's puzzle sought
God's gift to fill a lack

## God's Inner Silence

Mass opinion and facts can thus be likened
To the change of nature's perennial round
Just as foliage moves from lush to bare
The aggregate can foolishly shift and turn hell-bound
Both seem governed by an unknown force
Both appear not cognizant of their acts
Both change in concert and look the same
Both are blissfully ignorant of their lacks
But the 'forest' of confused and forlorn faces
Rejects the notion that they're spiritually stressed
But trifling lays to waste their sacred powers
It's why addictions and fads make them obsessed
The tension we seek to abate's repressed violence
The danger's in trying to avoid God's inner silence


## God's Our Best Protection

Modern day insurance is a plan
Under the benevolent guise, 'for our security'
The protection of our God, switched to man
A sullying of universal surity
Heaven and its hosts provide protection
For those who truly know and use God's laws
From the realm of wholeness and perfection
And done with nary an addendum or a clause
For every manmade system is after the fact
Really only to protect our money source
Security isn't ordered off some rack
It's wholeness found, from a heavenly course
Complete faith in God's our best protection
From life's arrows and spears, a real deflection

## God's the Truest Life Engraver

May each life be thought of as a mission
With no weakness pondered facing God
For with the wholeness of this inner vision
The soul can then see right through life's façade
There comes a time when on the spiritual way
We need to see the truth of God-potential
To externalize this power we must allay
All doubt and self-belittlement, most essential
Provided that the soul has gained humility
That one will thus attain a spiritual height
All attainment has its liability
The 'lording it over others' karmic* blight
This spiritual pride will cause a mighty schism
Defracting the radiance of our I AM prism

As part of the holy depth of illumination
Tied in with one's state of humility
Our path receives divine administration
Inexorably linked with our accountability
Revelation supports our personal charge
Impassioned prayer reveals our perfect plan
But one's experience in training by and large
Gives clues to how to serve our fellow man
While some in life will master many trades
Others develop one-pointedness in their call
Everyone's skill is revealed in different grades
But the highest attainment makes one master of all
All's unveiled to any found in favor
For our God's the truest life engraver

## The Growth of the Soul

So many in our modern day society
Are driven now by just one single goal
Worldly pelf and fame among their peers
When done, it's such a burden to the soul

193

It seems that all our God-given energies
Are spurred on as we struggle to attain
Higher position upon each other's shoulders
Chasing profit and a secular gain

Our best effort's in doing all we can
And our worst can also be the same
Is it based on a platform that is moral
Or a spiteful, joyless carnal game?

Striving for our wealth can cause disease
When driven by our avarice and greed
'Victories' won, no matter what the cost
Will not assuage our spirit's greatest need

The blest will use their talents and their gifts
Their attunement and their God-given drive
Improving life for many on this planet
Not to beat another or survive

Indeed the path they choose may sacrifice
A fine career, with its personal gain
But in their heart of hearts, they will know
That all their efforts made are not in vain

For how we're using any given talents
Our contribution to the human race
Will accrue as our manna set in heaven
Illuminate our spirit by His grace

Fervent prayer is exactly what will help us
To prioritize our day and our routine
Give us all the insight that is needed
To not be caught up somewhere in between

We then discover what's our truest purpose
Our dharma* and our future's purest goal
Not a worldly slave for worldly wealth
But a 'slave' for the growth of our soul

## Heavenly Ideation

Degrading to the term, mysticism
Is the prefix Christian, Islamic, Jew
For mysticism's pure from all distinction
The very core of heaven's sacred view
Though many become offended by a name
Others proudly wear it on their sleeve
Words are only good for fame or shame
Not for what we truly should believe
I am this or I am that means nothing
Nothing in the eyes of our one God
Unity of ideals is everything
Not standing behind a label's gray façade
Mysticism's a heavenly ideation
A source for understanding all creation


## His Mighty Plan

The only good things
Left after we die
Are the good deeds
That we have supplied

There's no glory and fame
Or wealth and cars
No power and charm
When we head for the stars

There's no deposit
Of gold and jewels
That accrues up there
But think not this cruel

For what is real
Never will change
But some human priorities
Are limited and strange

So much energy
Expended on what?
Just hoarding our toys
Our fast track's a rut

What is real
Good and pure
Not bought in a store
No pill that will cure

It's found within us
Far from the mall
This small voice when heard
Our clarion call

Listen, abide
To the way that is true
Take a close look
At life's review

How is life spent?
From morning to night
With loving action
Or maybe and might

We each are the key
God is the goal
A pledge and a plea
Strengthens the soul

Life's a real lesson
More than a book
Lovin' and blessin'
Can't be mistook

No time is lost
As our plan's unsealed
Constancy counts
As His light's revealed

We can Become
'Cause His way is grand
The total and sum
Of His mighty plan


## Hypocrite

A hypocrite is
One who sits
When preaching the virtues of standing
It's do as I say
Not as I do
'Cause talking is far less demanding


## Inner Prompts

The words of any language fall so short
Expressing inner peace
Trivialize and distort
Coarse utterances so profane
Lacking nuance and bluntly plain
The result's true understanding does decrease

As vague as the printed musical note
Clouding the big picture
Made so banal and rote
It's said "mere words cannot describe"
With true reality it does not jibe
Describing infinite truth, with finite stricture

The path of understanding's through experience
Using more than thought
Multidimensional nuance
When inner senses are employed
The more of truth is then enjoyed
These inner prompts provide the truth we've sought

## Just Uncork It

If our opinion turns
By what we've read
We can't say we think for our self
For within our soul
There's untapped stores
An infinity of heaven's wealth

If our opinion turns
By what we hear
Where's the source of our truth?
Kindled within
Is the fire of God
Just uncork it to imbibe living proof

## Life's Exalted Way

Wherever we may live
On this planet grand
Will present opportunities
Life's energies to command

With all these varied blessings
Come liabilities too
How they're addressed then shows
Us centered or askew

Those of us in the West
With abundance found so rife
Is 'the cart before the horse'
What's important in our life?

Materialism, idolatry
Extravagance galore
It's becoming so pervasive
Seems now it's just ignored

Takes us thither and yon
Past our center of being
Cacophonous noise and lights
Clouds true inner seeing

This becomes the measure
Of those who live in the West
Our desires running wild
Or a time to dispossess

Tossed now in the waves
Of materialism's sea
When 'things' become our god
We're truth's refugee

And those in the East
Whose reality is within
It becomes a myopic* path
Without earthly ends tied in

We're all here for a reason
Each of us, one and all
Not to shun this world
Bemoaning our primal fall

To create a heaven on earth
Stop living in the mind
It's a place for truth to flourish
Not becoming trapped and blind

A synthesis of truths
From all points on the map
Traditions so profound
Not the latest New Age trap

Time-honored protocols
Built on states of truth
Be it inner or outer blessings
The results are their own proof

In this period of decadence
The Kali Yuga* of world malaise
Everyone's an integral part
Blind rote is what delays

Ignorance of other cultures
Is a mindset based in fear
The twelve tribes of Israel
More alike than would appear

May each one live their life
By mastering truth's bouquet
Culled from East and West
It's life's exalted way

## Live a Life Profound

Immersed in such a glut of news each day
Isn't there any good done anywhere?
Day by day, it's messages of doom
This inundation's more than one can bear
Why's the daily news brought forth this way?
More good occurs each day than what we're told
But those that spend their time destroying life
Get headlines and become society's mold
Focusing on corruption, death and hate
Becomes a spiral to coarsen and debase
Every time it's spoken it acts like bait
The good that's there it slowly does erase
The choicest way of turning things around
Is turn off the news and live a life profound

## Moral Foundation

This generation of modern day vipers
Pushing their poisoned vanity with a beat
Turning sacred sound into profane
There's no light found in their foul conceit
Preening right across the modern stage
Fun and chaos is their calling card
Or decadence and a seething inner rage
And the gullible love to call them avant-guard
Controversial's now what we call art
To each his own is how it's all explained
Our naivete will tear us all apart
Calling anarchy freedom's now ingrained
Our moral foundation's lost within this maze
Without that standard, all our art decays


## The New Silk Road

What inspires the modern arts so sordid?
What spirit lurks behind their tainted veil?
Where and how did beauty get aborted?
Take a moment to hear this woeful tale
For surely there were points that tipped the scale
And individuals who ripped society atwain*
Deluging all, with their malevolent rain

In truth their sordid world's a house of straw
All they create's bereft of a spiritual sun
It takes our moral fiber and starts to gnaw
Leaves decaying carcasses, spent and done
How on earth could this have begun?
Who with sound and beat's expressing rage?
Hostile to the coming Golden Age

They're the soulless filled with spiritual pride
Peddling to the world their poisoned wares
Their cunning takes the innocent for a ride
One and all they are the biblical tares
Societal cancer's what their content bears
Their cacophony's the core of all our woe
How far will our freedom let them go?

Modern society needn't take this ride
Our slide to Gomorrah's not what God intends
Though we're free, can our hands be tied?
Where's the breaking point with what offends?
These toxic sounds, are the knife that rends
The danger's in our children thus affixed
Their souls, with this venom, are commixed

Our melting pot's become an astral* vat
Many seem just filled with human pride
But how to pull this rabbit from the hat?
And start to turn around this virulent* tide
How much more then can our culture bide?*
Doing nothing's at society's expense
Doing nothing's blatant negligence

There is beautiful music to behold
It's out there even in this present hour
Sources are both modern and quite old
Giving a modern renaissance renewed power
Through our cultural stench, a fragrant flower
Its cure will need to be then self-applied
A beautiful aural landscape to abide

These sounds of beauty, culled from every land
So many nations' people call this home
From these musics pure we can expand
Under this melting-pot's most sacred dome
Exquisite sounds create this aural poem
The clarion call is sounded with this ode
America can become the new Silk Road*

# One World, One God

Throughout the world's diverse religions
Our God is ever there
No burden on a devout soul
Not answered through a prayer

Souls throughout this blessed planet
From every race and creed
By all their prayers and affirmations
Find comfort in times of need

God requires no mosque or temple
No church or synagogue
He only needs a sincere heart
To start a dialogue

Though we upon His glorious mountain
Each walk a unique path
We need to love our fellow traveler
Not upon them send our wrath

For as we each surrender to
God's plan for our life stream
We will know without a doubt
His truth is no pipe dream

This coming age, all people sense
In their heart of hearts
Is something that each soul shall see
In time as God imparts

The dogma of the modern faith
In each and every land
Has lost the true connection with
His cosmic divine plan

Instead we see fanatics spew
A trite simplicity
Perverting all that's truth and grace
With our complicity

This call goes out to God's true souls
Spread across this earth
Instead of seeing our differences
Seek within for a re-birth

Our God can go by many names
They're labels we have spun
Don't let superficialities
Block our victories won

A common ground is what we'll need
To get ourselves on track
Only when we search within
Is abundance found, not lack

Take some time to call to God
In whatever language used
Ask Him to be awakened 'cause
A pure heart's not refused

## Our Birthright

The debasers of this nation will unseal
Vials of darkness leading to our fall
As cults of death destroy our youth piecemeal
Our heritage is stained, we're found AWOL
Consider the havoc of this vile onslaught
Upon our country built with patriots' lives
Could their stalwart courage be for naught?
With indifference, can this land survive?
If people are to rally to the cause
Their prayers need faith to counter this adversity
For victory's not attained beyond God's laws
To stem the tide of darkness and perversity
If God's the core of what we do believe
Complacency can never thus deceive

Invested is mankind in mortal dominance
Releasing untold misery upon this world
As we see our loss of rights by ignorance
Indulgence is the bane that we've unfurled
As this nation's inheritance slips away
Trashed and stepped upon, we know it not
We'll never mourn the loss till judgment day
But who's behind this diabolic plot?
No longer do we treasure inherent rights
As those of freedom's birthright just stand by
By awakening mastery with a just foundation
We'll know the standards to exemplify
Understand the power of people free
It's our birthright, bestowed by God-decree


## Our Culture's Holy Leaven

Music's always been the noblest art
Passed on down through every generation
Somewhere we the people did depart
From what was pure, in its captivation
An arcane* view revealed by inner source
For millennia it's been the art divine
By disconnecting from God it lost its course
See its lineage to see its slow decline
For eons it has been a door to heaven
But a lot of it today's a hatch to hell
It's now no more our culture's holy leaven
The state it's in is sonically unwell
When will people see the 'sound' connection?
Our tastes in music need a resurrection

## Our Spirits' Burdens

It's time this country wakes up to reality
To see the errors that sway this nation's soul
Too much energy's expended in vain banality
As we lose this nation's central goal
Wishful thinking will not clear the slate
With our collective heads stuck in the sand
No action is the fruit of more debate
As this bastion of freedom's left unmanned
The war for every soul's 'tween light and dark
View the nightly news if there's a doubt
Social ills are now our watermark
But know it's waged within not just without
Materialism and frolic won't assuage
Our spirits' burdens in this present age


## Prayer and Supplication

When we pray to God
Know it matters not
Where that prayer is done
Just the fire we've got

No pantheon of worship
Or ritual that's heeded
But a heart sincere
Becomes all that's needed

Occuring in an instant
Or taking ordained time
What's crucial is our presence
Not the chant or rhyme

Communion with our God
Take's on a cast of forms
But this can not be codified
In orthodoxy's norm

The standard to be met
Begins with supplication
Our expression just won't work
With formalized recitation

Only words within
Can fully bear the weight
To penetrate the deepest
Let spirit invocate

There's a wisdom garnered
And protection gained
But this heavenly contract
Is never pre-ordained

Only fervent prayers
Or pure of heart decreeing
Penetrates deeper layers
Of our very being

Quickens and awakens
With a holy fire
Wisdom's truest seeing
What all may thus acquire

The purest forms of contact
Need no words at all
But a focused pure heart flame
Is what does thus enthrall

Infinite potential's
What our communion's spun
But state thus: "Not my will,
Let only Thine be done"

## Reawaken Our Destiny

When faith that's true does turn to mere belief
And rural lanes to alleys in a city
When wisdom pure becomes a man-made kef*
Such a nation earns our grief and pity

When they're no longer making what they wear
Or growing wholesome food that they will eat
Sustaining cultural arts with their devotion
Then that nation's destiny's sure defeat

How could a nation free subdue itself?
Seeing perversion as a noble strain
Idolizing what steals its innate wealth
As truth and freedom spiral down the drain

Sacred rights and freedoms will not last
When placed upon a shifting human sand
A culture that has 'popped' has all aghast
Replacing good with evil throughout the land

Bureaucrats', diplomats' enchainment*
With changing truths, based on human will
Whose industry and desire's entertainment
Its culture so immersed in toxic swill

Pity a nation countering outside enemies
With symbolism and a host of trite cliché
Offensive is whatever's not P.C.
Shouting down free speech is thought OK

Sad, is the nation, with voiceless sages
Its champions and its heroes spiritually blind
The self-proclaimed prattler is who engages
Centered in a fad not truth-aligned

The end is nearer for a sovereign nation
When all its tribes, claim their special rights
With forced re-distribution of its wealth
Upheld by the government's power and might

You may ask, how does such a nation
Conceived with liberty and justice for its all
Allow such a poisoned ideation
To sweep the land and lead to its downfall

With so few untouched by a tainted truth
And even fewer set to take a stand
The days are numbered for this blessed nation
To reawaken each woman, child and man

The way for such a nation to survive
Is for every citizen in their soul
To seek the moral ground that would revive
The flame of freedom that they should extol

Only at that time will such a nation
Disentangle from its fun and mirth
To reawaken the destiny God ordained
Through its founders, at that nation's birth

### Search for Truth

Why is every life a different length?
Some, well beyond the century mark
While others never make it past their birth
There's more here than just simple luck or lark
If all of us have been created equal
By the God professed in every creed
Then why do all these things seem so unfair?
There's more than meets the eye, we must concede
The answer is we've all been here before
In concert with God's law and sometimes not
All our debts to life must be repaid
That's how we have right now just what we've got
Good works will raise our spirit ever higher
Breaking cosmic law's our burdens' sire

It's true that we are all created equal
For most, that was many lives ago
By our acquiring the sense of good and evil
The Golden Rule makes our state apropos
The talents or afflictions we possess
We've earned through many lives, near and far
For all our good and bad does carry over
Creating now, exactly who we are
Our soul remembers every single life
But most, consciously remember very little
The more in alignment with God's will we are
The more He'll give us answers to this riddle
Search for truth, till the heart's at peace
When ready we'll receive His full release


### The Sense of Innocence

Our souls' sense of innocence has been cut off
Throughout this blessed land and across the world
The joys of purity and the child-like mind
Have fallen as intellectualism's been unfurled
The sweet, innocent heart attuned to nature
And to God within has been aborted
For the sophistry and complexity of our age
Our inner senses have slowly been distorted
By the forceful taking of our innocence
And the enthronement of the carnal mind
Its worldly desires have purged the Golden Rule
And slowly made us all now spiritually blind
Our world's no longer dwelling with the Lord
Nor He in temples human hands have poured

## Setting a Standard

To qualify to vote's no racist test
For voting's a sacred privilege that should be earned
Mob rule is what we really must arrest
An uninformed democracy must be spurned
As we reduce our voting qualifications
We lower the ethical standards of our leaders
A society bereft of civic education
Gets empty candidates peaking voting meters
Elections exist to hold the elected accountable
An essential key to keep a free society
Our corrupted state is sad, and lamentable
Brought on by elitists with their faceless piety
Elections will beget what we deserve
But will the elected defend, and preserve?

A confused elector blithely goes to vote
And what's the principle sought from coast to coast?
The quality that many voters seem to note
Is who will give the greatest to the most?
The only way of getting 'round this curve
And giving this nation's future a fighting chance
Is if we the people find backbone and nerve
To stop our voting 'the wallet in our pants'
When candidates no longer buy their seat
By putting a 'moneyed' smile on our face
Then other views may jump in and compete
With 'lifers' finally moved out and replaced
Only with a standard to then vote
Will this nation's freedom stay afloat

## Singing Our Life's Song

What's our greatest gift to offer life?
Where do all our varied talents lie?
Does our service rendered speak of love?
If so, most any gift will qualify
For many, life is taking and not giving
Self-absorption's become their twisted way
All life seems to owe them, but not vice versa
Their carnal mind is all that they'll obey
The way that all we do can ever glow
With a feeling of fulfillment in our heart
Is to know that what we do will better life
With the goodness that each day we will impart
Our calling can be seen as right or wrong
Depending on how we're singing our life's song

## Spiritual or Mortal Gain?

The loss of mortal things becomes a gain
A gain in the immortal spheres of life
Awakens the soul asleep in carnal stain
Pursuing worldly pleasures found so rife
But renunciation for gain is only greed
The pleasure of itself is what's worthwhile
Our souls surrender to this holy creed
Helps it soar above what's base and vile
There is no worldly gain without a loss
Be it money or our valued time
We need then to decide just who's the boss
Pursuing worldly things or what's sublime
All spiritual gain is counted in forever
Our free will says just when we'll pull the lever

## Standing for the Truth

In standing for the truth within our heart
How much then are we willing to reveal?
Motives found sincere set one apart
Fearlessness decides what we'll unseal
For all our God discloses, needs be taught
Flow's the natural order of His plan
We're the voice and hands for what He's wrought
Be enflamed with His love and take a stand
The compass of our platform He'll disclose
He sees our inner motives with lesser things
Our depth of love and meekness will expose
The truest source from whence desire springs
The more of life we willingly surrender
The more light God will offer to engender

## Take Our Stand

As myriad forms of death unfold each day
Revealed in all our avenues of news
One wonders why such darkness is on display
Was it always this blighted hitherto?
In truth now these end times have unsealed
A lid that's been upon the astral plane
The poison of these serpents, now revealed
As levels of 'the pit' are being drained
Last chance, for these lost ones to be found
But verily hell on earth is their desire
That's why the darkness seems to so abound
The fallen ones are breathing their hell fire
Those of the light must finally take their stand
Proclaiming victory now throughout the land

## Then vs. Now

To peruse the beautiful tomes of the past
The purity of their transcendent vision true
These delicate etchings of their souls will last
Touching the resplendent life all may pursue
The innocence of these distant bygone ages
Clashes with the absorption of our day
Pearls of wisdom from near and distant sages
A safe harbor from the hardened way
Such beauty in the art, poem and psalm
A legacy upon the falling sands of time
Where've we as a people free gone wrong
To create such decadence from this source sublime?
Without a reverence for what's whole and true
Only a human decline can thus ensue


## There's No Half Way

May the church of life be built
Upon the cause of souls who know
Who've been through deepest, darkest times
And know, now's the time to grow

They are convinced without a doubt
There's no time to wile or waste
To build a pyre of sacred fire
Poisoned water they'll not taste

No more veering right or left
Life's path is straight ahead fore're
For time is short, each moment counts
Climbing up life's cosmic stairs

Contemplate the book of life
Know what's sacred and profane
Where'er attention's now been placed
Becomes the world that we sustain

Every erg of energy used
Winds up upon this side or that
When one is up the other's down
There's no state in life as flat

If human stuff is where we're at
Then what's sacred's on the wane
No care is paid to temporal ways
God's light is what we surely gain

Every moment through all time
This hallowed principle's in play
Be aware, you'll tip the scale
In all of life there's no half way


## Things Are Now Our Master

Never met a sale you didn't love?
'Bargains' empty the wallet
Of what we had thereof
Stocking up becomes corrupt
Things are where our light's tied up
And tomorrow we'll buy a better 'whatchamacallit'

Products are never designed to satisfy
Materialism's become our god
A never-ending supply
Nothing's created to endure
So future profits are ensured
Buying a happy life's our sad façade

Industry is the torment of our soul
The newest and latest sell
But desire takes its toll
Consuming has no satisfaction
Simply just a God-distraction
As sales and ads continue to compel

Better, newer, cleaner, cheaper, faster
Advertising's art
But things are now our master
Spend and spend, we're happy now
Until the new sale anyhow
Buying happiness poisons our very heart

An artificial reality's what we've built
Ego gratification
Based on greed and guilt
What now, pray tell, will sell and sell?
We're bleeding dry our spiritual well
Things will never lead to our salvation


**This Prying Eye**

The less you watch the tube the less you need it
Consciousness wraps itself 'round other things
By tending other fields you start to cede it
Reaping the abundant harvest that this brings
Mindless inaction's the legacy of TV
Participation in life then slows to nil
Attention atrophies till we cannot see
The box's schedule replaces inner will
A plethora of variety leading mostly nowhere
Movies, cartoons, 'how-tos' and our sports
Twenty four by seven, all life's bare
With talking heads and piles of new reports
This prying eye leaves not a stone unturned
A deluge of information that's unearned

## Through Love

Our modern day world
So cynically cold
Power and greed
Our society does mold

To take a stand
When all without
Darkness and fear
And war all about

God's love is bigger
Than races or creeds
Is omnipresent
Filling our needs

God bless our world
With radiant light
Restoring wholeness
To make things right

For only Your blessings
Can give us a chance
That we as a world
Through love may advance


## To Live Forevermore

If we sense that we have eaten
We've probably eaten too much
Now the body's spent and beaten
Food's our emotional crutch

In this nation of abundance
We obsess too much on food
Most of eating's based in ignorance
Platitudes, trite or crude

What many now call sustenance
Has wandered far and wide
We're in a dietary trance
What's true we don't abide

Tampering with our food abounds
Not allied with our source
But any diet pure and sound
Free societies can't enforce

Habits that began in childhood
With sugar, fat and salt
Science now defines what's good
Our pride is what's at fault

The holistic knowledge of the past
Has bowed to parceled study
Few will play the iconoclast*
Our habits shaped like putty

Light and whole's the proper fare
To put us back on track
But food's become a huge affair
With ads that never slack

Quelling our throbbing hunger pang
Is all we think to do
We'd best prepare for malady's bang
Bad habits will accrue

Addictions have a 'wellness' price
Begot from ignorance's way
Those ads will tug and so entice
Starting health's decay

Our tastes are what have headed south
Foods from an impure source
We'll only care what's in our mouth
When we feel remorse

To realize how we can do better
And learn the power of food
No longer dietary jet-setter
Indulging in plentitude

God has planned it from the start
Our needs from earth and sea
Has made us now a vital part
Of this divine decree

In living by His sacred plan
With diet at the core
We'll fulfill the dream of man
To live forevermore

## To Science

Science, the bastard child of wisdom whole
Altering the purity of God by human mind
Our future's just a part of what you stole
Like an oarless ship you search purblind
Your highbrow eye can see no God-reality
For 'superstition's' not the empirical way
But searching with a template of duality
You've got no moral scale on which to weigh
By twisting cosmic law you set in motion
Riptides sent across our matter plane
The academic's where you find devotion
Creating your own reality seems insane
Without an anchor in your soul that's real
Your 'nuts and bolts' approach will not congeal

## Toll Upon the Soul

There is a sacred flame within our heart
That needs protection with our very being
For it's a jewel with secrets to impart
Don't let outer coarseness cloud true seeing

This outer world kicks up a mighty wind
Enough to smother out this holy taper
Creates a darkened cloud as if we'd sinned
Good feelings disappearing as a vapor

For this filigree of angel-woven light
Commences as a delicate web of joy
A sensitive heart attuned by inner sight
Is easily coarsened by a carnal ploy

Communion with what's sacred helps one find
The purity of the spirit's innate tone
But all the crassness of the worldly mind
Hardens the heart as if it's brick or stone

Indulging in life's astral sea of woe
The bottomless pit of all that does debase
Abusing anything in life will sow
A darkened spirit lacking heaven's grace

The carnal mind creates a hardened shell
Where all that's whole and pure just cannot be
The delicate way of truth the soul dispels
Desires create an eye that cannot see

The danger in this whimsy of the world
And its voice within that leads us on
Is all of God-reality is thus furled
And the light that we expend, forever gone

By parting with the outer world's quagmire
And its ways impinging on the soul
A communion with the grace of sacred fire*
Keeps our soul attuned to the end goal

Indulging there will dampen inner glow
It's more than harmless time to get away
In truth, it's more the shovel and the hoe
That digs the hole,
That takes its toll,
Upon the soul

## True Religion

The truly pious have no denomination
For true religion's how one lives one's life
Orthodoxy's become a corporation
Throughout the world, their venues found so rife
These different sects exist for just one thing
For few to hoard the light of many souls
The salvation they espouse will never bring
Their faithful closer to eternal goals
Our journey back to God is made alone
Alone, but ever wound up with His presence
Aspiring to our final steppingstone
While taking on a 'godly' luminescence
No sanctioned faith can e'er bestow this blessing
From noble starts, they've all now been regressing

## Truth and Honor

There is a glory and an honor true
The glory of our service fully done
The integrity and the honor of one's virtue
And of noble victories fought and won

Public and private life should e'er be cast
By the same exalting moral code
These marks of truth and honor then hold fast
To the high way of the 'straight and narrow' road

## Truth and Mercy

Diligence is the price we pay for liberty
By reinforcing faith in one another
Desisting from our senseless carping rasp
This maligning may be our nation's final gasp
Not grounded in the strength of perfect love
But an errant sense of human judgment
An authority that's not ours, so beware
If we're judging life, anywhere
Let mercy be our first consideration
Justice is always secondary to it
As mercy graces equality in our world
The truth that's found in all becomes unfurled
For truth and mercy form a matrix whole
Let them be our active spiritual goal

## Two-Edged Sword

How can mankind truly know their freedom?
Without a moral base, all is lost
Debauchery in lieu of holy wisdom
The path of truth and light is what it costs
We the people took the carnal lie
Compromised the truth within our souls
The result is many now won't even try
Illusion animates our sordid goals
Our gift of freedom weighs upon us all
With it comes responsibility's trust
Disciplined self-restraint becomes the call
A base of moral virtue a must
Anarchy's a 'freedom' that's abhored
Know Freedom is a moral two-edged sword

## Union Without Unity

Union without unity
Not the way to go
Like tying cats together
No harmony and no flow

Our nation's in a fix
Through lack of common sense
The melting pot's been cooled
At unity's expense

Immigration today
Not how it used to be
The purpose always was
A desire to be free

Now so many come
To live off others' backs
Of those who earn their way
The 'haves' support the 'slacks'

Our melting pot's language
Is English through and through
Without this base to work from
We'll Balkanize, it's true

If those who wish to come here
Believe in freedom's flame
However they are different
Is less than what's the same

Without the firm desire
To help this nation grow
Their motives then are suspect
It's poisoned seed they sow

That statue in our harbor
Does liberty proclaim
Not seeking our free hand-outs
Her message put to shame

It's said we shouldn't ask
How this land can help us
Instead, what can we do
To earn this nation's trust

Our country welcomes all
With open arms and heart
If you truly desire
What freedom can impart

To all, their full potential
Following each one's dream
A universal vision
Not a socialist scheme

Rugged individualism
Is how this nation grew
Come here to live this dream
And honestly accrue

Then we can fulfill
Our founders' special vision
A union based on unity
Not a social fission*

God's the very basis
For the founding of this land
The cornerstone of freedom
What makes this nation grand

If all who touch these shores
Would live the Golden Rule
Our nation would be the standard
As heaven's peerless jewel

## Unity of Religious Ideals

The danger found, on this mortal plane
With those who answer not to heaven's law
Is a world beset by tension, war and pain
By those who hold world governments in awe
The brotherhood of man can never rule
Without a connection to a higher source
Their authority then is out of touch and cruel
A single governing group, their chosen course
A base of humane ideals will not be found
Regardless of which elite does run the show
There'll always be major contrasts that abound
And get-even's not the right scenario
The unity that needs be nourished on this earth
Is one of religious ideals, a true rebirth

## Urban Flight

The harshness of the urban landscape felt
A burden and a bane upon the soul
Losing the innate in which our race has dwelt
The antithesis of our ever becoming whole
Pollution, noise and constant degradation
Abut 'shrines' to the success and ego cult
The coarseness of a puny imagination
Moral degeneration, the result
A myopic view of self and of the world
In a land of cocksure attitude
The 'poisonality' of life has been unfurled
Displaying a mien that's hyper, short and rude
Urban flight's indicative of our age
The spirit needs a far more peaceful stage

## Valid Proof

Life is but a constant push for gain
The difference is in the type that it may be
No matter where our soul is on this plane
All gains in life, start with mastery
But consider, is our yield for God or mammon?
What we attain requires inner vision
Regardless if our gain is feast or famine
Nothing is more grave than this decision
Really, how can profit be called good?
To gain the worldly but to loose our soul
Build not upon a basis of falsehood
Just use your heart to ascertain the goal
For wealth can be a poverty in truth
How we feel within's our valid proof


## Vibration

All in life emits a vibrant sound
Though physical manifestation's not apparent
We hear so very little of what abounds
Some vibrations dense and some transparent
Color and cycles both emit a pulse
Above and below our human aural range
Vibrations either settle or convulse
And cause a corporal-spiritual interchange
If outer senses had more scope and reach
We'd then hear color and see a sound's vibration
In truth, we do a little bit of each
All outer phenomena have a sound relation
Vibration is both physical and supernal*
Our connection with the now and the eternal

# Victory on Life's Page

Behold the modern waxen god
Melting before the carnal flame
Few know Spirit's staff and rod
Buying the lie is what's to blame

The modern message is profane
Only one savior for us all
Alternative views held in disdain
No other path, no other call

Diluting such a concept pure
Idolatry of a human form
Platitudes just won't be the cure
Or condemning what's not seen as norm

We're each endowed with a cosmic spark
The eternal flame of God within
So many wander in the dark
Missing all that could have been

There's not a single other person
With the power to save our soul
Rejecting truth can only worsen
The chance to ever reach life's goal

Bickering over doctored tales
Not the way of the Prince of Peace
Becoming the timeless flame unveiled
Is what then gave his soul increase

"Why callest thou me good?"*
Should really make it very clear
No glory to his own selfhood
Only God within hold dear

Passion for what we feel is true
In time will only go so far
What's left unanswered is a clue
There's more unknown now to his star

He set an example for our age
Of how to live a life that's right
Showed what happens when God's engaged
Living beneath His eternal light

He said that we'll do "greater things"*
For he's returned now to the Father
The fact that we're an equal stings
Putting the hidebound in a pother*

How can what we do be greater
If we're of a lesser light
He was a consummate educator
Ageless example of what's right

Jesus is part of a Brotherhood
A Brotherhood of radiant light
Ascended legions pure and good
Their home is also our birthright

They've set examples East and West
Examples of what we all must do
The path for all to gain access
As we become what's real and true

All are blessed with this Spirit spark
As all avatars and saints
By following the way of this hierarch
We're transcending life's constraints

Walking the path that Jesus did
Along with every saint and sage
We're building our own pyramid
Acclaiming victory on life's page

## We Can't Buy Happiness

We try to buy our happiness
In boxes of materialism
This blitheness is elusive
A petty form of surrealism

For things won't make us happy
No matter how we try
Fleeting prompts and nudges
Of memories when 'knee high'

Back then, we quickly realized
A toy could make us smile
Back then we had no clue
It would only last a while

Will we start to realize
Our elation's not unfurled
Until we know ourselves
In relation to God's world?

## We The People

How'd this nation forged in patriots' blood
To proudly become so bountiful and free
Deteriorate in a resounding socialist thud
To now become the 'nation of the fee'?
With intentions good the plea is made
Tugging at the heartstrings of this nation
Next, the guilt-trip is the standard grade
As slowly 'good' deteriorates to negation
Money cannot heal a burdened life
Or guarantee success in any calling
No peace is found but many forms of strife
Unless one 'earns', their life is slowly stalling
Taking's how a government gains control
"We only want to help", its protocol

## We're Guided and Awakened

Sophistication and dependence take their form
From knowledge gleaned right from the outer world
For many a generation it's been the norm
As inner wisdom slowly becomes furled
Standards false have led us for too long
Placing awareness on a physical course
Impious, vain conjecture's tired song
Will we ever doubt our "experts'" source?
We're each a chalice for a purer wisdom
A perfect science that our God has wrought
But a sophist pride will have its preferred outcome
This fallacious bill of goods that we have bought
We're guided by our power to receive
We're awakened by our power to believe

## We're Responsible!

We're responsible for who we are
Where we're at in life, so far
And if our soul's been helped or marred
We're responsible!

We're responsible for making change
When viewed up close or from long range
The lesser for the greater exchange
We're responsible!

We're responsible, don't pass the buck
Divinely spun, not whimsical luck
Stop stepping in life's mire and muck
We're responsible!

We're responsible for our pains and joys
For what gives pleasure or annoys
To disentangle from human ploys
We're responsible!

We're responsible for victories won
To stand fast now or cut and run
To know our life's what we have spun
We're responsible!

We're responsible to get up and go
Dynamic victory or meek and slow
Dropping off or continuing to grow
We're responsible!

We're responsible for what we partake
To what's not healthy, applying the brake
With all we do it's for His sake
We're responsible!

We're responsible for what we become
Each jot and tittle, the total and sum
To awaken and live with grace and aplomb
We're responsible!


## When the Heart is Right

There's more to life than livelihood and goods
Buying leisure has its other side
Fame and fortune are life's great falsehoods
The core of these is always human pride
Don't get involved with any type of venture
That denies the doing of God's business
In so doing, life's a misadventure
It goes to the quick* of what we call success
Any work has something we can tweak
If not, then find the one that speaks within
Let talent and interest affect what we would seek
Finding our true calling's a win-win
Cast with heart flame all is rightful station
When the heart is right it's God's creation

## When Will We Learn?

Pollution from light and sound's a bane of life
For the one that seeks an inner dimension
Bombarded from without with modern strife
An anchor's weight upon our soul's ascension
Mankind's 'progress' mars the inner way
Scars and coarsens intricate waves of light
So hard to keep these psychic raids at bay
Indeed it needs to be our spiritual right
For these are others' audio-visual intrusions
Endlessly slamming our ethereal auric* field
Fewer living spaces are now exclusions
It's time that some expansion is repealed
Modern convenience is dulling inner growth
When will we learn we really can't have both?

## Why Fear Sells

So many live their lives in subtle fear
Though when asked, most would sure deny it
But reality and our feelings don't cohere
Our obsession with the negative signifies it
What's outpictured daily in the news?
Or the results of scientific research
Outcomes of not filling Sunday's pews
Trepidation's voice is on its perch
Fear is what's the motivating factor
The result of all this negative proselytization*
These prophets of doom are God-reality's detractors
The outcome of a limited rationalization
It's time to stop and examine why fear sells
And our poisoned culture it parallels

232

## Wisdom's Knife

Listen to experience
There's wisdom that's intoned
Whether rocky or smooth
It's bred deep in the bone

Persistence and discipline
Experience always shows
The keys to our success
Reaping what we sow

Wisdom becomes the victory
Of accord over illusion
Desire creates all bondage
Deception and delusion

There's courage and inner calm
When confident and ready
Wisdom's the clarion beacon
To becoming true and steady

All who have lived life
Have attained some insight
By never closing doors
Those pieces then unite

The highest and the lowest
Outplays throughout all life
If we open our heart
We'll attune to wisdom's knife

## Write Boldly on Life's Page

As one sets the Christ example
That others may then see
Those souls in time, will be strengthened
To find they too can be

It's by the raising of our consciousness
With motives whole and pure
Life's dimensions become limitless
When our soul's secure

Making contact with our God
And drawing forth His plan
Inventions or the cultural arts
To raise the plane of man

By staunchly rolling up our sleeves
To bless what life presents
What to life may we best offer?
Impacting its events

We each have a true potential
To perfect our gifts
Our mark unique's then placed on life
The power of love that lifts

By applying all that we've been given
With heart, head and hands
Love, wisdom and power are balanced
As each quality expands

Let skills be honed and set in concert
For the enlightenment of our age
As full potential's realized we'll
Write boldly on life's page!

# 4

# Creativity

## A Wake-Up-Call

Music's potential's a beautiful meditation
An open door to heaven's glorious way
Its essence is the core of all creation
Its power's in its potency to sway
Hence, caution is the byword in its use
It's much more than a peripheral, mindless game
As our society out-pictures its abuse
Today's perversions will eventually seem tame
For those who corrupt and poison know its power
It's the needle shooting the drug of twisted minds
These thoughts are really not extreme or dour
But a wake-up-call to see the danger signs
Music's an essential reason societies change
In what direction will we set our sight and range?


## Creating Arts Divine

A sensitive artist's soul should wander free
Throughout the halls of Spirit's infinite love
Beholding etheric beauty by His decree
The perfection of cosmic law that's held above
This is the way of nature's shaping archetype
All is of a subtle concord made
Nature's beauty's fashioned whole in spite
Of a world that's cast in mist and shade
Study the nuance and the endless variety
Of flowers and the tall and beautiful trees
Then acknowledge with a humble piety
Manmade's never arrayed as one of these
The highest vibration is of a pliant soul
Creating arts divine, life's highest goal

## The Creative Mindset

Our mental space is really all that counts
We're the ones that shut or tap the flow
We each will yield at varied grades and amounts
An inspired life is what we then self-sow
By making a subtle adjustment in our head
Whatever's done is endowed with God-potential
At first it's not as easy as when said
But creating the mindset's what is most essential
Being aware, right now right where we are
An ideal step for anything we do
Sensing all experience as on par
Means less experience that we will eschew
Maintain the creative mindset all the time
Whatever's done is then more full and sublime

## The Creative Spirit

Creativity's as a walk on newfound trail
Experiencing what surprises are in store
How it's walked brings out our talent grail
Life's artistic spirit's from our core
Do we just maintain the beaten path?
With not a thought of alternate lanes galore
And what's retained in each walk's aftermath?
Attunement tells us take in or ignore
Does this experience relate to others past?
Know beauty's found in more than eyes and ears
How long does that creative spirit last?
Sense more before you than just what appears
Alertness and an imaginative fire impart
The full creative spirit, from God's heart

# Crux of Our Problem

Music's harmonics are part of heaven's law
Woven then within our cosmos whole
Western music decreed that it knew better
By tweaking natural harmonics on life's scroll
Our even-tempered scale produced the 'dot'*
And made each musical 'gap'* now sound exact
Keyboard harmony is what it all begot
Not leaving the natural tempered scale intact
For eons, global music's followed nature
The music created reflects these laws within
Western music claimed its way superior
Its progeny's placed us in a downward spin
God's laws allow a music that's unfettered
Why do humans think it can be bettered?

# Does Practice Make Perfect?

Practice makes one perfect
Is true up to a point
When done with rote repetition
Our gains will disappoint

The flame of inspiration
Is kindled from within
How strong is that connection?
Is set ere we begin

Studies thus repeated
While we're somewhere else
Congeals imperfection
Tosses substance for the shells

A slow, focused attention
With our mind on what we do
Results come so much faster
Full potential to imbue

The quality of practice time
Is shaped by inner sense
The time to then move on
Is felt at rote's expense

Diversions in subtle guises
Are to test the focused mind
The joy of sensing potential
Pure effort, without the grind

Focus begets precision
Born in a methodical brew
Not charmed by lots of notes
If their source is just not true

First ask, what inspires
To practice every day
With our motives true
We'll discover mastery's way

### Dots on the Page

To all of those who use
Their eyes to learn to 'hear'
A practice in Western music
That's held so very dear

One needs to know all music
Indeed is actually sound
Not a radical thought
But still one to expound

You see, if all of music
Is an aural art
Then why do dots* on a page
Play such a vital part?

It's because our music's source
Has essentially been lost
The inner spark to create
Has now been all but tossed

In our not so distant past
Improvisation reigned
But dots on a page
Have now become ingrained

We're told by academia
They've deciphered the past
And know how these grand masters
Wrote music that would last

But all those 'rules' discovered
Were fathomed after the cause
Their spirits were the source
Not intellectual laws

And the source of all those dots
Now read on scores and pages
Were created as they improvised
In all those bygone ages

Modernity's cadenzas
Scripted 'perfectly'
Back then were just spontaneous
And that's the essential key

Today's virtuosity
Is mostly just skin-deep
For years of living's needed
'fore one can truly reap

A most important aspect
Not taught but more reviled
Those great composers were
All truly then self-styled

Each of us can draw on
This same creative Muse
That latent, pure potential
We all can tap and use

Creating one's own music
Should start off right away
With a favored instrument
Let joy come into play

If one should ever doubt this
Here's some food for thought:
Many of our great artists
Were principally self-taught

Now take this one step further
When speaking through the day
We create our thoughts unplanned
No text to help convey

But always thus remember
The source of musical sound
Is in us, not without
Where inspiration's found

This apothem* of old
Is still so true today
It makes a crucial point
When in our heart we weigh

We'll no more create pure music
From dots upon a page
Than create a beautiful painting
With a coloring book as our gage

## Flowing Spontaneity

Perfection is an expanding improvised art
Musically adapting myriad situations
Allowing the higher mind to then impart
Heaven's realm in ever-expanding gradations
Single-minded purpose is how to live
Especially when aligned with higher will
What part of us we'll sacrifice and give
What void will we creatively then fill?
Improvisation's a synchronistic flow
Opening doors that previously went unseen
The creative process in which, all things grow
Where the soul emits a radiant gleam
A flowing spontaneity shows the way
As life-long improvisation, day to day


## Life's Musical Realm

The beauty and variety of our world's music
Are branches of a mighty cosmic tree
Each so unique, but still connected
Their origin's in a heavenly pedigree

The Music of the Spheres*, is our source
Of all the sounds drawn forth from higher realms
It's the trunk and sap of all this musical wealth
Creating a variety that nearly overwhelms

But as it is in all of natural creation
Disease can literally destroy it from the core
The world's musical realm, has its toxins
No matter how much they're loved and adored

For all of life has sound as its source
Patterns of geometric beauty and perfection
But rhythm not aligned with divine law
Blurs and distorts this heavenly reflection

There's a pulse of balance, from stars to atoms
Unfolding this perfection throughout life
When it's disrupted through our strident sound
Chaos and anarchy result by aural strife

For every being surely has a motive
That affects the 'life-tone' they bring forth
If not aligned then with the cosmic order
Their waves of imperfection will distort

As any carrier of malady or of strife
Can on the surface seem a mark of health
So too, can a society abrim with fortune
Carry germs of destruction hid in stealth

Before it's fully revealed to all apparent
It's reeked its nocent* poison from within
Destroys our society with a moral turpitude
Irregardless of all our ignorance and spin

The germ cell of this 'plague' that threatens life
Has its source in the music we embrace
We're each the cells, of this planet body
Do we glorify life, or just debase?

## Making Life More Royal

Scholarship will never forge true art
It's a pedant* shadow of what's true and real
The one that emphasizes academics
Won't sense what intuition can reveal

Our inner voice won't ripen in a class room
The soul's not nurtured in this atmosphere
True art won't flower with a business mindset
A route pursued through ignorance or fear

To have revealed one's inner voice and calling
Takes a firm and disciplined search within
Years of focused practice and refinement
Overcoming frustration and chagrin

The path of less resistance is one's schooling
Degrees sought after in an art career
One's inner voice is mostly never touched
Becoming versed in styles of yesteryear

Though studying tradition can be found most fruitful
A structured class will never be the place
For each one's motivation is unique
This matrix which school rigors would deface

Our personal muse can easily be snuffed out
When practicing contemporized clichés
With mastery of a 'played to death' score
No freedom for a soul that dreams and strays

Discover what you love and then pursue it
That vision brings one through the toughest time
To touch your very core will build momentum
A higher aspiration, so sublime

Every soul's unique and can create
Endowed with all tradition's fertile soil
If the voice we find is touched by heaven
Our art's a blessing making life more royal

## The Molding Power of Genius

Know love, as the molding power of genius
Bringing forth what's hidden, mum or dormant
One's inner senses aligned to higher purpose
It need not be with self-imposed torment
When aligned with heaven's love and law
God reveals His beautiful perfection
Our Higher Self creates sans human flaw
From realms of light beyond sensate detection
The beauty and perfection found in art
Is showing if that one's aligned or not
Inspiration from His blessed heart
Slowly stewed in our sensorium* pot
Genius is a melding not a 'stroke'
Through His creative fires, that we stoke

## The Music of Life

We know there's sublime music, in the pluck of the lute
And a beautiful dulcet tone, in the melodies of the flute
There's music in all things, if we'd purify our ears
All that we hear in life, is but the echo of the spheres

For all the sounds we hear, have their natal source
Depending on who we are they'll sound soothing or seem coarse
Just how they move us, is determined by who we are
With our inner ear we sense, the beauty or bizarre

Most don't think the sounds of life, could e'er be called a song
But if you were to hold this thought, you know it would be wrong
What we all perceive as music, has its start within
Takes its shape, in our minds, as structured sound or din

As we grow and search for truth, from each and every source
We start to learn surrender, the right way to plot our course
The more we can encompass, as life's instruction for our soul
The more we'll know the sounds we hear, are important to our goal

Wholeness from within creates, all wholeness found without
We decide what to take in or reject, it's done without a doubt
Percussion, strings, flutes and voice become, organized, a matrix heard
From the infinity of sounds, we decide what's preferred

The level of attunement of, who makes these sounds a song
Coincides quite literally with those, of like mind, among the throng
But who's to say who's wrong, and to say who's right
To each his own is what we're told, though this seems quite trite

The more imperfect the concepts held, by those who hear the song,
Does place each soul, on life's path, moving up or down ere long
Perfect or imperfect thought, draws in more of its kind
This applies to all the arts, what's within is what we find

Our awareness of what's beautiful, is more than happenstance
It goes to the very core of what is truth or ignorance
If those who create the music, think of life as carnal game
Then that's what they bring forth, burdening life, and truth defame

Unless we as a culture strive, to raise our consciousness
We'll continue to lower standards down, the pit that's bottomless
There's no better place to start, to heal our spiritual strife
Than to know the kind of music that leads, to truth, a renaissance life

## Order or Chaos

Music molds and shapes us and society
It weaves its patterns in our very cells
Are they ordered patterns or of chaos?
The type of sounds we listen to will tell
Dissonance and jagged pulse distorts
The pure resonance of our inner world
We need just take a look to see results
It's plain to see our souls are thus imperiled
Ingesting impure food and impure sound
Starts a pattern heading for decay
Until we stop and fathom the connection
We're on a slippery slope, straight away
"Garbage in, garbage out" is what we're told
Input does affect what we ensoul

## Our Full Potential

Only perfect practice makes one perfect
In the arts or simply in our day
With 'no one home' we'll simply not detect
The moment from perfection that we stray
Ideals present an ever-expanding goal
No earthly ability can touch that hallowed ground
God still puts that image in our soul
Anchored in His wisdom, pure and sound
For our determined effort helps us true*
With His perfection seed that's found within
But human doubt and fear can block our view
To His inspired will, we're not akin
Our full potential can unfold, it's true
When by divine perfection we're renewed

## Our Spiritual Culture

Wouldn't it be a wonderful thing
If every single soul would sing
A song of beauty, joy and peace
To sing a dulcet* sweet release

How we lead ourselves each day
Becomes a 'song' that we portray
A magnet for God's light above
Blessing life with heaven's love

All we hear then thus accrues
Magnifies or dims virtues
They're steps composed of sacred fire
Designed to take us ever higher

Music's in concert with our mien
What goes in is what we glean
Who's the creator of that song?
A way to know what's right or wrong

For music mirrors perfectly
The type of fruit from that one's tree
Pure or tainted, source the trail
Their 'sounds' define them in detail

Music that is pure will sway
Create a culture ensoleil*
Impure music when it's traced
Shows decay, a world debased

We're transformed by sounds we hear
Becoming what goes in our ear
The purest music God has crowned
Is where our spiritual culture's found

# Pure Gifts

Technique can be a two-edged sword
Expression's means or how it's buried
When lacking heart it's just discord
The soul is where our creation's juried

Profound beauty will have a core
A pure connection with what's real
Technique gains access to the store
As personal mastery will reveal

No one's connection's quite the same
But Spirit is the constant source
The shimmer of this cosmic flame
Illumines each soul's chosen source

The means of expression will unfold
Will beckon with its vision clear
Personal mastery will then mold
Help disparate parts to then cohere

Awakened stillness to create
Heart-seeds sown in grounds of feeling
The budding of a germ innate
Its nature then more self-revealing

But devotion that's not always heeded
Must stay the course of light discerned
Visions pure are never ceded
It's how a culture's ways are turned

Mastery's from the inside out
Not ever from the outside in
But shadows cast of fear and doubt
Shroud one's instinct to imagine

Art like life requires time
A nurturing of the budding flower
Music, painting, dance or rhyme
Need years to harness depth and power

Life experiences sculpt technique
Limitation contours form
Shapes and molds a voice unique
Lore* recast and thus reborn

Perfection is a shrouded peak
Illusive is the path that's true
All have varied means to seek
And different talents that accrue

Self-knowledge is the certain way
Of unveiling full potential
Our personal muse will then convey
The core of what in life's essential

Those who touch infinity's realm
And cultivate a voice of love
Have Christ-command then at the helm
For all pure gifts are from above

**Sacred Inner Fire**

Kundalini* enhances inspiration
Wisdom, intuition and the arts
A connection with the heart of all creation
Stirring latent talent, what it imparts
Filled with joy, the body glows with peace
Not mired in a course of human bane
With discipline, this glow can then increase
The soul has touched a new and higher plane
To take the inner eye off God within
Drops this energy to what's base and low
Perverting a state that always should have been
The vital core of how our soul does grow
This sacred inner fire is our birthright
The spark of God's wisdom, love and might

## We're Endowed

Since 'part' of God is anchored in the senses
And part is anchored in our heart and soul
A penchant to see on through life's hidden fences
Kindles inspiration, the aspirant's goal
The place where soul and senses intermix
Is the cauldron of our creative sacred fire
To find that space is how conception clicks
And how an endowed vision is acquired
This gift's for all, not just the chosen few
Persistence and forthrightness are the key
God presents imagination's cue
We need to Be, before we hear and see
If we're part of God, the great creator
Then we're endowed as more than just spectator

## What our Culture Needs

Take a look at all our printed music
Both classics and the modern well-loved song
Where else in life is sound reduced to print?
There's something here that's manifestly wrong
For music is a language without words
Deep expressions of the heart and soul
The eye can never take us to that place
If touching another's heart-flame is our goal
Eyes will codify thinking and the outer
Ears embrace the beautiful inner world
The only way the West can find it's balance
Is study how the ancient arts unfurled
What western music needs to emphasize
Is anyone can learn to improvise

## What We've Become

We'll not apply to any art
Something that's not inside
There's really no way to impart
What the soul has not supplied

Experience in a life lived long
The storehouse that we draw from
Without it, there's no art or song
The truth of all that we've become

# 5
# Love & Relationships

## All That We Keep In

A family's memories are a sacred trust
Varied images of love, pain and joy
Keeping them in the heart becomes a must
With all the special love one can employ
For these thoughts, in time, are all we keep
Many feelings of our kinfolk few
Recollections settle very deep
With all emotions gathered hitherto
Over time, these thoughts seem sad or sweet
Depending on our purpose to resolve
Bruises thus sustained need not be beat
Allowing life's relations to evolve
There's no one we've known longer than our kin
Let loving thoughts be all that we keep in


## Be the Quenching Cup

The breath of purest being is the essence
Of God's Spirit, indeed a holy thing
This wondrous breath's the Holy Spirit's presence
An inducing of the triune flames to sing
By meditating on purposeful intent
We draw the soul to heaven's inspiration
To sing, starts to bind and heal all rents
Focusing the plan of each one's incarnation
The pure expansion of power, wisdom, love
Demands the curbing of our human pride
Watch and pray, to our God above
To know when truth is lawfully applied
Be the quenching cup to all you meet
Naught in life's intrinsically as sweet

## Being Feminine

A woman's vulnerability's a part of innocence
A blessing and pure aspect of her being
But acting helpless has a consequence
Showing a lack that's binding and not freeing
Vulnerable and feeble are of a different thread
One of inner strength and one of weakness
Self-restraint's the path one needs to tread
The balance found is part of your uniqueness
For those who can perceive the bigger picture
Will ultimately see the way of give and take
Not abiding in society's defective stricture
But living a life that's quickened and awake
Being feminine, not feeble, is the call
God has graced you with the wherewithal

## The Bonding of Two Hearts

To loose someone you love creates such pain
For a life together's the bonding of two hearts
But know that in that time of inner strain
The love created is stronger when one parts
Common memories are precious to behold
They live forever within the heart and mind
Though one is now beyond this life's threshold
Those thoughts become more beautiful and defined
Let the bond between your souls be strong
For each pure love's indeed a blessed shrine
May the comfort accorded all life long
Be poured upon all pain as love's sunshine
If the one set free is in your heart
Then know your souls will never be apart

## Brotherhood of Unity

It doesn't matter where we live
But how we live when there
Let radiant peace and love exude
Tempering carnal glare

We become the bastion for
Life's abundant way
A holy, precious, radiant love
With means to then convey

The place and time to carry forth
Our calling on the path
Has direct relation to
The attunement that we hath

For where we live or who we see
Has many karmic ties
The balancing of the laws of life
To everyone applies

Let no one ever take for granted
The blessings life presents
The inner way makes plain to all
The meaning of events

Any souls we come upon
We've met in lives before
Will we bless with truth and love?
Or triflingly ignore?

The simple act of love and kindness
With a respectful mien
Sends waves of good throughout all life
Not energies that demean

We all can make a difference with
Each soul we come upon
Opportunity has its time and place
And then forever gone

Make each opportunity count
Within our ways and goals
Their wholeness felt within will be
Our vow to life and souls

As we're striving every day
To show ourselves approved
Take trite, petty, human things
And let them be removed

God does work with souls of light
To help them serve His plan
Makes each one a focus for
His love poured out to man

Give thanks to all of life each day
For the gift of opportunity
There's now the chance to help create
A brotherhood of unity

## Cultivate the Truth

A word's a chalice for a thought or feeling
To thus express what's in one's heart or mind
Wisdom pure is ever more appealing
Found in the love of Spirit so sublime
By finding inner peace before we speak
And purifying the mind before we say
Harmony becomes the core of what we seek
The essence of the pure and holy way
How we play the 'drum' of each one's ear
Flowing forth or as a jagged thump
To cultivate a peaceful atmosphere
The choicest way to prime another's pump
Be the voice of God throughout the day
Cultivate the truth in all you say

## Dreams Come True

There is a dream I know I had
Both beautiful and rare
The dream of every mom and dad
Like an answered prayer

The reason I'm sure I had this dream
While holding one like you
Now gazing at your eyes agleam
I know that dream came true

## The Flame Within Each Heart

To enter the coil of one's transformation
We'll rise upon our views of life and man
For all contains divinity's germination
But most don't know their truest breadth and span

Where'er we find a soul that we would blame
Whatever rung of life they stand upon
They have a light that's cast as threefold flame*
Not our place to judge their fate foregone

Cast no stone upon another's way
Know God's truest test is of humility
By bowing 'fore the flame within each heart
God aligns our heart and our civility

## From Our Heart

There's just a single type of love that counts
The one that gives with no desire to get
For if there's expectation when we give
Frustration's what results, and inner debt
For love that is immortal always knows
Giving in itself's a pure release
A release that ever blesses and ever grows
And fills the giver with eternal peace
If that's the type of love that we would give
There's nothing we could need then in return
To give becomes the only way to live
The most essential lesson we can learn
When through our heart God's love we now dispense
His love returned becomes our recompense


## The Gems of Life

A woman is to any man
As light is to a taper
She illumines his trying world
Transcends life's mists and vapor

Nurtures his supernal gifts
The mortar of his foundation
Holding varied things together
Allaying his frustration

Turns his dreams to wakefulness
His wakefulness to dream
Knows the secrets of his heart
Sets his soul agleam

Cast from father Adam's rib
The better half by far
A cherished, blooming, sacred rose
Love's endless reservoir

Thank you God for our dear women
Life's civilizing grace
Their loving and most delicate presence
Life's gems that we embrace


## Generosity

Generosity creates warmth both far and wide
A glowing from a blest magnanimous heart
Giving goes against the current tide
For many are self-absorbed and found apart
The generous heart will look for opportunity
A wealth of possibilities every day
The world's a portion of their hearts' community
Expending self completely, their forte
Contemplate just how this world would change
If everyone would take it on their self
Give their worth within their sphere and range
A mending of this planet's spiritual health
Being aloof opposes generosity
Which dims our spirit's potent luminosity


## In the Presence of Our God

May we be no burden on another
There's still so much that we alone must do
Discover and to know about our self
All the sacred truth we must accrue

But when devoting all our time and energy
To things we really have no need to know
We're missing all those special opportunities
Life's wisdom gleaned that helps our soul to grow

The energy lost, when it's focused on
Life's soap operas, raging near and far
Like molasses in a jar of coins
Becomes a dense and darkened psychic tar

There's a lack of nobility in one's character
Indulging in this vain and worldly prate*
To speak behind an unsuspecting back
Life finds ways to then reciprocate

It's said, "Judge not, that ye be not judged"
Sound advice brought forth from one who knows
All we say then will reflect upon us
By unwisely allowing this habit to grow

When speaking ill of any individual
We're building up a hefty karmic* wad
For even though we're speaking in their absence
We're speaking in the presence of our God

### The Karma of Fair Play

Listen to all that people say
Observe how people act
For in this wide, mixed array
We'll see us so exact

We're all possessed of similar traits
They're either good or bad
Some obfuscate*, some obviate*
It's how some souls are clad

There's quite a wealth of special insight
Life lessons to be learned
No one can teach us everything
But no one should be spurned

We'll see in everyone observed
The spectrum of our race
From worst to best and in between
An instructive interface

For every soul we meet's a teacher
Of what we should or shouldn't do
To go within, our conscience says,
"I see me there too"

Our higher self then makes it clear
What part will truly work
The world reflects all values plain
To embrace or what to shirk

Mastering the art of right and wrong
We first must pause a spell
Decide if where we're at right now
Will allow us to excel

When not the case, observe those souls
Who cross our path each day
What they believe is what we see
For all is on display

When we study life and people
Perceive with our ability
Absorb or reject what we observe
Our base starts in humility

We'll soon know we're responsible
For where we stand each day
There's no one else to ever blame
It's the karma of fair-play

### Language of the Soul

Plant no barren seedling as a tumor
Dejection, dark as night, upon one's heart
But preach the gospel of a sense of humor
Raise the sides of mouths, as a works of art

For burdens are carried with us every day
Whether real or perceived, it matters not
A heart-felt smile helps troubles to allay
Trails of hope and joy are what's begot

For smiling is the language of the soul
Understood no matter where we're from
If unity upon this earth's to be our goal
A brotherhood of smiles, first must come

## Life's Pure Way

Life's pure way's the path of truth and silence
Seeing, but not casting judgment's fire
For burdening others is a spiritual violence
Not fit or apt of those who do aspire
The Middle Way* embodies special tolerance
Live and let live is its sacred code
Our place in life is judged by our forbearance
Criticism adds weight to another's load
View all souls as giving life their best
Perceiving any lack's still where they are
To hold the tongue, then becomes the test
To then expand our full ascension star
Patience found through tolerance is the way
Expressing love, His law to thus obey

## Mirror of Life

We shall remain as strangers still
In this life we call our own
Each unto their lonely self
Who we are, to all unknown

Until the day when you shall speak
And I with open heart do listen
To hear your voice as if my own
Then God's way I'll truly christen

For at that time with you before me
His vision to my soul restore
I'll know without, reflects within
This mirror of my soul adore

## Mother

Mother is the word behind creation
A word of love and wisdom from the heart
The cornerstone of every soul's foundation
To all of life a blessed vital part
Source of consolation 'mid all sorrow
Strength in weakness, misery's constant hope
A sun upon the gloom of every shadow
Protectress of her brood that they may cope
Everything in nature speaks of mother
Our celestial sun is mother to the earth
The earth with all its glorious verdant cover
Sustaining life beyond our physical birth
Mother is the paradigm of love
Omega's tangible flame from above


## Only Love Survives

Purest love's the garland of eternity
A fragrance wafting through the paths of time
But in this day of self-imposed modernity
We've turned our backs on what we know sublime
We grasp at things in life for sentient comfort
To mollify frustration, fear and doubt
But habits and addictions just contort
A vision pure to know what life's about
There's no more beautiful virtue to imbibe
Than the aspects of God's purest love
So beautiful, yet difficult to describe
A bouquet of light descending from above
Live not the broken covenant that deprives
Our heart's assured, only love survives

## Path of Truth

Stoking regenerate fires in the soul
Pouring it out as embers in the heart
The heat dissolves partitions into whole
The glow will raise a soul up and apart
To all our fellow travelers on life's way
A ray of victory gleams within the eye
Hope and joy to all the world convey
With peace that's deep which naught can thus deny
How joyous and expectant is God's hope
When turning from a flawed and sinuous path
A proactive life is never duck or cope
But rising above life's worldly sin and wrath
Become a light ray for a darkened world
As the path of truth becomes unfurled

## Pyramid of the Ages

Pay rapt attention to your real self
The doorway to reality
Reveals the secrets of the saints
Done with impartiality

By truly lifting up the veil
Upon all ages past
Seeing service that was rendered
By those who held steadfast

They ever glow as mighty stars
In all the bygone ages
Even right until this day
Their way leaps from life's pages

They each embodied their true self
In each deed and word
Their stands for freedom and for truth
Luminous not blurred

We each of us must also build
Our pyramid from love's scouth*
Rising from life's desert floor
To the apex of full truth

With examples of life's chosen few
Build your pyramid well
With it's footing set in love
Not desires cast pell-mell

Then we each can also be
As history's saints and sages
Towering above life's arid sands
Truth's pyramid of the ages


**The Title "She"**

O gender fair, endowed with precious grace
Flower and filigree thread of all of life
Omega is God's aspect you'll retrace
Whether mother, daughter, sister, wife
Nurturing is your sacred gift to bless
Whether kin or 'cross this blessed earth
To mother, counsel, comfort or caress
You're the presence for this world's rebirth
The civilizing force, found within creation
The balancing charge of Spirit's pure descent
In the Tai Chi of this manifestation
You are Alpha's perfect compliment
Divinity's cast upon the title "She"
"S" is for what's sacred joined to "He"

## What's Most Essential

Do newborns really start with a clean slate?
As a blanket white of virgin snow
Then what we 'write' will surely mold their fate
Our guidance helps their infant souls to grow
In truth, they're really not a spotless slate
More a safe with many hidden riches
Not a point of wrangle to debate
But a concept known that so enriches
The preceding generation needs to find
Passkeys to unlock their very soul
For all have access to their higher mind
When will this be parenting's highest goal?
If we unlock our children's full potential
We have then achieved what's most essential

# 6

# Nature

## Awaken to Fulfill

O nascent dawn within each lovely heart
Does stir anew to quicken and expand
This sun, the same ablaze in everyone
As each soul arises in its land
As the sun each day is newly born
In lands across this lovely verdant earth
Creating a cosmic ring of endless dawns
Awakened in each daytime's new rebirth
What is this fire ablaze within each heart?
From whence, does it find its common wellspring?
Its source, is indeed the same as dawn
The Sun behind the sun in everything
Be quickened now, quickened by God's will
His dream within, awaken to fulfill


## Back to Nature

Our soul's at home, living in the country
The rural life is living in God's home
The urban milieu begets stress and tension
It can't compare with nature's halidome*
Steel, mortar and glass distort God's light
The resonance of the soul with higher realms
This man-made savage cage of sin and blight
Suffocates the soul and overwhelms
Trees and mountains, grass, hills and plants
Nourish the soul in poignant ways unseen
Communion in this shrine of open air
A pure and holy covenant so serene
Our urban jungles will not soothe the soul
Back to nature's what will make us whole

## Become God's Love

Fire, air, water and earth serve God
Though to us there seems no life within
In truth there's life behind our world's façade
His love enkindles all that's ever been
Elements are varied levels of crystal light
Expanding as a mighty cosmic burst
The soul aligned, does expand in spite
Of the whole in which we are immersed
All that is within us is without
No portion of existence is exempt
As the soul taps into heaven's spout
It sees a world that one has only dreamt
You and He and we and all are one
When we become the love that God has spun


## Creations of the Mind

On a quiet morn or a quiet night
When the sky is clear and all's agleam
Find a place devoid of man-made light
And gaze upon the dome of sweet star beams
Pick a single orb from out the span
Meditate upon its celestial place
Nothing's changed since God created man
The megacycle of interstellar space
Still, contemplate that single ray of light
Its distance and its size so truly vast
But all considered, it shines above 'in spite'
It may have ceased to be in distant past
Time and space are creations of the mind
God's and ours are beautifully entwined

## Dawn

New morning from its eastern womb aflame
First glint of light behind the verdant hill
The crown upon horizon's marge acclaim
Silver to the starlight it doth still
The glow of new creation through dawn's chill
From the void as forms become defined
Broken silence by the pre-dawn shrill
Answered back and forth as all opine
An exquisite pageant at this daybreak shrine

Great clouds ignite in pink, celestial hue
Feathered choirs heralding the new day
Animated as if by cosmic cue
All of heaven's glory on display
Each new panorama won't dismay
Rays of light illumine the massif
Choreographed as nature's true ballet
Diverging shades and light, a grand motif
Sooths the soul to strengthen our belief

## Eventide Stroll

Oh, pre-dawn saunter
Post-dusk walk
Why do I love thee so?
Thy ebony quiet
Stills all thought
That my soul may grow

Each day's bustle
Drawn without
As contemplation's lost
Responsibilities
Fray sensibilities
My peace of mind exhaust

But most of all
Not one sun's rays
Upon me when I'm done
I'm always blessed
On eventide strolls
With many a thousand suns


## Inner Dimensions

Stars are but the sparkling of angel's hearts
Cast across all space in light array
The blessing that this message should impart
A star is added on our ascension day
Each orb's nightly glow is but a beacon
The blessing of a sacred internal event
The supreme expression across the eternal eons
The edict of another soul's ascent
They are the one example in our life
To witness the past in our illusory timeline
The ancient glitters before us every night
In our Father's inviolate pure design
Astronomy is our limited avenue
Bringing inner dimensions to outer view

## Mother Nature

Be nourished by the sanity of nature
The beauties of its calm and gentle ways
Attuned to its special nomenclature*
It's comfort till the end of mortal days
Mother is the term so often used
Listen to the cures she will impart
Brings clarity to the soul that is bemused
When burdens have us down, it's where to start
Calms amid the welter of sensation
All chaff 'fore nature's wind does surely fly
Opens the heart, to its revelation
All turbulence in our world demystify
When nature casts her spell upon the soul
Our lower bodies* gain unity, blest and whole

## Nature's Retreat

Nature is a retreat for inspiration
The dwelling place, for our higher Self
Such beauty that our soul may then mature
The natural world exudes its sacred wealth
Creation helps us see the life of things
All's alive and everywhere there's song
Spontaneity amongst its perfect order
It's truly where our heart and soul belong
The vastness and the stillness is a comfort
Quiets all our inner stir and toil
There's something far more deeply interfused
A oneness with the sky, trees and soil
The soul is one in Mother Nature's womb
As our higher virtues start to bloom

## Pastoral Overture

Beautiful, majestic, rock-edged, craggy peaks
Jutting high above a placid lake
This image pure upon our soul thus speaks
Such beauty painted for our spirit's sake
Fir and aspen edge the rippling stream
Serenity in the chilly mountain air
Billowing sentinels now no longer screen
The 'golden eye's' dear warmth that all may share
Surely this is God's cathedral grand
Restoring wholeness to a weary soul
One's at peace within this primal land
Recharging with each footstep of a stroll
Nature always has the perfect cure
Healed within its pastoral overture


## Pre-Dawn

There's beauty in the stillness of pre-dawn
All's subdued to let the heart increase
In these 'spiritual hours' the soul has drawn
Closer to her* source, the God of peace
The world is dormant, quiet and asleep
This stillness allows the inner to expand
Before our responsibilities then upsweep
As the awakened dawn does fill the land
Quiet and dark without, draws one in
Where outer experience needs to get its start
As heaven's glow and feathered songs begin
We'll find we live our day more in the heart
Dawn is how our God begins each day
Pre-dawn is when to meditate and pray

## Summer's Full-Blown Glory

The most wonderful of our estival* events
Is the opening of the 'panes of separation'
The true significance of what this represents
Is the allowing in of nature's pure vibration
The innerving sound of every living thing
Is nature's music, to each quickened soul
The blessing that the rustling leaves do bring
Is enhanced by the song of oriole
The open home then wafts with nature's peace
Is more at one with heaven's healing mien
This blending with the elements does increase
A calming oneness felt with what's unseen
The magic of the summer's full blown glory
The apex of creation's etern story


## Universal Order

We are found rewakened and restored
With spring's dawning insights in the land
More than flowers and leaves to be adored
But the healing of the soul, a therapy grand
Nature's awesome tapestry's thus combined
With cycles emanating from our core
In truth, it's all created in our mind
Not something to fluff off or just ignore
For each and every season is a part
Of the infinite order of the ages
Birth, growth, yield and death impart
What's been known by venerate* saints and sages
Spring's the start, each year, of seasonal flow
The starter 'yeast' within life's cyclic 'dough'

# GLOSSARY

| | |
|---|---|
| **Abrogate** | To put aside, annul |
| **Aegis** | Demeanor |
| **Amity** | Accord, friendship |
| **Anathema** | Curses |
| **Antecedent** | Preexistent |
| **Anthropomorphic** | Ascribing human attributes to something |
| **Apothem** | Short, instructive saying |
| **Appentency** | Appetite |
| **Arcane** | Understood by very few, esoteric |
| **Arcane** | Known by very few, secret, esoteric |
| **Astral** | Psychic level below the physical in vibration |
| **Attar** | Perfume |
| **Atwain** | Archaic: In two, apart |
| **August** | Grand |
| **Aura, Auric** | Energy field around all living things |
| **Avatar** | Hindu term meaning embodied master of life |
| **Avower** | Open declaration |
| **Bale** | Archaic: Woe, misery, sorrow |
| **Bide** | Archaic: Endure |
| **Bodhi Tree** | Fig tree in India, under which the founder of Buddhism attained enlightenment |
| **Bodhi** | Supreme enlightenment |
| **Caprice** | To change one's mind without apparent motive |
| **Causal Chest** | The Causal Body is the habitation of the Spirit of the I AM THAT I AM to which the soul returns in the ritual of the ascension. Our spiritual resources and momentums of good works are stored there and may be drawn forth as our treasure laid up in heaven. See Matthew 6:20. |
| **Chakras** | Sanskrit word for wheels, denoting seven spiritual centers aligned along the spine |
| **Chi** | In oriental philosophies, the vital force within the body |
| **Chimeric** | Imaginary |
| **Cleave** | To adhere closely |
| **Collateral** | Aside from the main course or direction |
| **Confluent** | Flowing together, blending into one |

| | |
|---|---|
| **Cosmic Clock** | Cycles of tests and initiations in life that start at one's birth |
| **Crystal Chord** | The stream of light and consciousness from God that sustains the soul |
| **Cupidity** | Excessive desire |
| **D**eftly | Skillfully |
| **Dharma** | Hinduism, Buddhism: The essential quality or calling in one's life |
| **Diadem** | Crown |
| **Die** | Cast or mold |
| **Dictum** | An authoritative pronouncement |
| **Dot** | The printed musical note |
| **Dowry** | A natural gift |
| **Druthers** | One's own way |
| **Dulcet** | Pleasant to the ear |
| **Dweller** | The Dweller on the Threshold is an accumulation of all that is not God-oriented within us. |
| **E**lide | Ignore |
| **Embay** | Enclose |
| **Enchainment** | To bind, confine, restrain |
| **Energism** | The theory that self-realization is the highest good |
| **Engird** | Encompass, surround |
| **Enmity** | A feeling of ill will |
| **Ensoleil** | Surrounded by rays of light |
| **Equipoise** | Balance |
| **Estival** | Pertaining to summer |
| **F**ateful | Having momentous consequences |
| **Fission** | The act of splitting into parts |
| **Foison** | Abundance, abundant harvest |
| **Forefelt** | Perceived beforehand |
| **G**ap | The interval between musical notes. The even-tempered scale made all these intervals, except the octave, a little out of tune to compensate for the 'discrepancies' of the natural tempered scale. That brought about Western harmony, but many believe it contrary to nature's laws. |

| | |
|---|---|
| **Gird** | Prepare |
| **Greater Things** | A quote of Jesus in the New Testament. See John 14:12. |
| **Guise** | Form, shape |
| ***H*abiliments** | Clothing |
| **Halidome** | A holy place |
| **Her** | The soul is always the feminine counterpart to the masculine Spirit whether in a male or female body. |
| ***I* AM** | I AM, capped, is the esoteric name of God as in I AM THAT I AM. Whatever follows "I am" is where we pour God's light. |
| **Iconoclast** | One who attacks cherished beliefs that are based on error or superstition |
| **Immortelle** | An everlasting flower |
| **Insular** | Detached, isolated |
| **Involute** | To curve or spiral inward |
| ***J*ihad** | Any vigorous crusade for an idea or principle |
| **Jobbery** | Public business for the sake of improper private gain |
| ***K*ali Yuga** | Hinduism: The fourth and present age of the world, characterized by conflict and sin |
| **Karma, Karmic** | A tenet of Hinduism and Buddhism. All that we've done, both good and bad, returns to us. |
| **Kef** | A state of drowsy contentment, especially from illicit drugs |
| **Kundalini** | Hinduism: The vital force lying dormant with in us until activated by spiritual disciplines |
| ***L*ese Majesty** | Attacks on customs and beliefs held sacred |
| **Lore** | A body of traditional knowledge |
| **Lower Bodies** | Plural, representing our physical, mental, emotional and spiritual "bodies" |
| **Lumined** | Archaic for illumined |
| ***M*acro** | Short for Macrobiotics |

| | |
|---|---|
| **Macrobiotics** | The science of enhancing life through a natural diet adjusted for age, sex, lifestyle and geographic location |
| **Magnanimity** | Generosity and nobility of character |
| **Mantle** | Our gift, our highest manifest potential |
| **Mastication** | Chewing |
| **Mayic** | Hindu term meaning illusion |
| **Mean** | Average |
| **Mendacity** | Deception, lies |
| **Middle Way** | Buddhism: The path towards enlightenment avoiding extremes |
| **Milieu** | Sphere, setting |
| **Mite** | A very small object |
| **Moil** | Confusion, turmoil or trouble |
| **Monad** | An indivisible entity that is a microcosm of the universe |
| **Music of the Spheres** | Imperceptible to the outer ears. Produced by the 'vibration' of the movements of the heavenly spheres. |
| **Myopic** | Narrow minded, intolerant |
| ***N*ascent** | Beginning to develop |
| **Nescience** | Lack of knowledge |
| **Nimbus** | Halo |
| **Nocent** | Injurious |
| **Nomenclature** | Language or terms comprising a system |
| **Not-self** | The illusory human ego |
| ***O*bfuscate** | Muddle, confuse |
| **Obviate** | Avert |
| **Om** | Hinduism: A mantric word believed to be a complete expression of Brahman (God) |
| **Omniscient** | Perceiving all things |
| **Overt** | Plain, apparent |
| ***P*athogen** | Disease-producing agent |
| **Pedant** | One who rigidly adheres to book knowledge, overemphasizing rules |
| **Pedantry** | Excessive display of learning |
| **Petulance** | Irritability and touchiness |
| **Pine** | To suffer grief and regret, languish |

| | |
|---|---|
| **Pother** | Commotion, uproar |
| **Prana, Pranic** | Yogic term for the vital energy moving within the body derived through breathing |
| **Pranayama** | The science of breath control, consisting of exercises to develop vibrant health in body and mind |
| **Prate** | Empty or foolish talk |
| **Progenitor** | Someone who indicates a new direction |
| **Propagate** | To increase in extent |
| **Propriety** | Decency, rightness, justness |
| **Proselytization** | To convert or recruit |
| **Puerile** | Of or pertaining to childhood |
| **Purgation** | A cleansing or purging |

| | |
|---|---|
| $Q$**uick** | Most important part |

| | |
|---|---|
| $R$**asp** | To scrape or grate |
| **Rasping** | Grating, irritating |
| **Ray** | See Seven-hued |
| **Renunciation** | Abandoning or sacrificing something |
| **Replete** | Filled, complete |
| **Reproved** | Corrected, admonished |
| **Reticence** | Disposition to be silent |
| **Rue** | Regret bitterly |

| | |
|---|---|
| $S$**agacious** | Wise, discerning |
| **Scouth** | Abundance |
| **Sensorium** | The sensory channels of the body |
| **Seven-hued** | Seven colors, corresponding to the seven chakras, have aspects of God qualities attributed to them: blue/power; yellow/widom; pink/love; white/purity; green/healing & truth; purple/service & peace; violet/freedom and transmutation. |
| **Seven Sacred Jewels** | See Chakras |
| **Silk Road** | The ancient Silk Road was the trade route from the Far East to the Middle East, where the arts and cultures of many lands commingled. |
| **Single Eye** | Called the Third Eye, the basis of intuition |
| **Sinuous** | Meandering, having many curves |

| | |
|---|---|
| **Smite** | To impress |
| **Somatic** | Having to do with the body, physical |
| **Sundered** | Separated, divided |
| **Supernal** | Heavenly, celestial |
| **Symbiosis** | Interdependent relationship |
| ***T*emporal** | Worldly |
| **Tender** | To submit something for acceptance |
| **Threefold Flame** | The spark of life, anchored in the heart, manifesting as love, wisdom and power. The goal of a spiritual path is to balance and expand these attributes. Most people are stronger on one and weaker on others. |
| **Throes** | Struggles, turmoil |
| **Tripartite** | Father, Son and Holy Spirit |
| **True** | Adjust exactly, align |
| ***V*enerate** | To regard with reverence |
| **Viands** | Dishes of food |
| **Vicissitudes** | Changes |
| **Violet Flame** | Also called the Flame of Transmutation, the seventh ray aspect of the Holy Spirit. |
| **Virulent** | Malignant, deadly |
| ***W*hy callest thou me good?** | A quote of Jesus in the New Testament. See Mark 10:18 and Luke 18:19. |
| **Wont** | Custom or habit |
| **Woof** | Texture |
| **Wroth** | Anger, turbulence |
| ***Y*e are gods** | A pronouncement in the Old and New Testaments. See Isaiah 41:23, Psalms 82:6 and John 10:34. |
| **Yin and Yang** | The oriental principle of opposites in life (female/male, cold/hot, contracting/expanding) |
| **Yin** | In the Macrobiotic system, Sugar-based food is considered Yin. |